Traditional Dahlia Quilt *(pattern begins on page 7)*

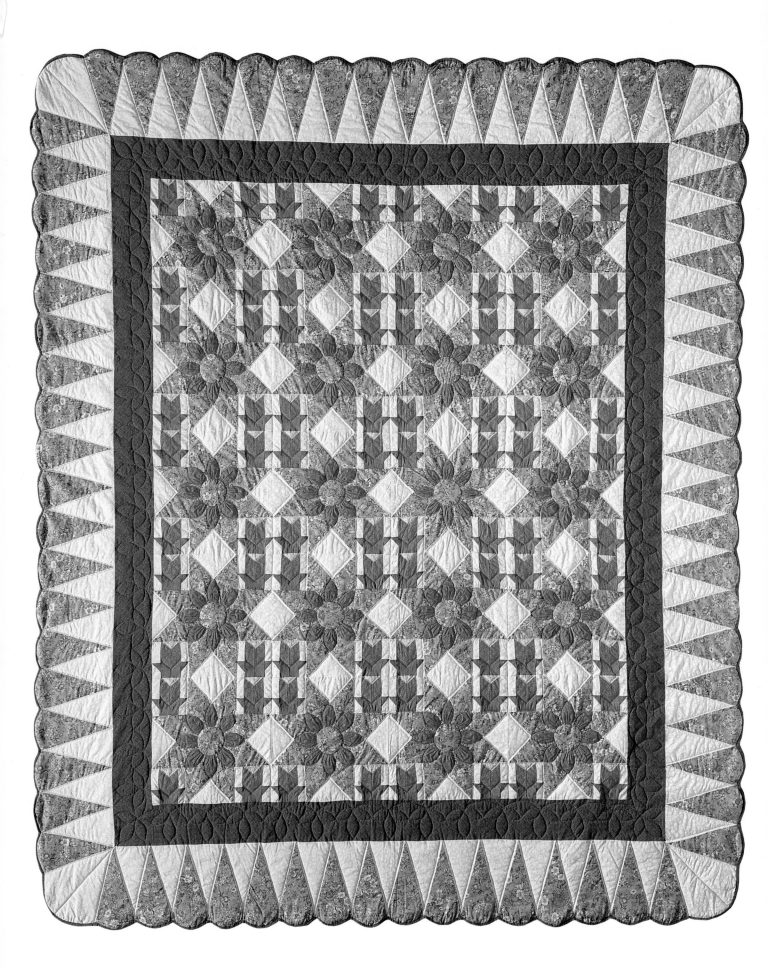

Dahlia and Tulip Quilt *(pattern begins on page 23)*

DAHLIA QUILTS and PROJECTS

DAHLIA QUILTS and PROJECTS

Cheryl Benner

Rachel T. Pellman

Good Books

Intercourse, PA 17534

We are grateful to the Dahlia quiltmakers in our neighborhood who advised us, and skillfully and efficiently worked with our patterns to make the completed projects shown in this book.

We have done our best to provide patterns and instructions that are accurate and understandable.

Fabrics and individual skills vary, however. Therefore, we suggest that you study each project carefully in its entirety before beginning.

Good Books assumes no responsibility for losses or damages resulting from information given in this book.

Design by Dawn J. Ranck
Cover design by Cheryl Benner
Photography by Paul Jacobs, Charles Studio

DAHLIA QUILTS AND PROJECTS
© 1995 by Good Books
International Standard Book Number: 1-56148-179-3

Table of Contents

About the Dahlia Quilt Pattern

The Dahlia pattern is based on a traditional geometric eight-point star, but it takes a distinct diversion from tradition by adding curved, puffy, gathered petals and a round center. These variations on the basic geometric design make the assembly of the patch more difficult. The compensation for that extra effort, however, is a stunning quilt in three dimensions.

The Dahlia quilt has been popular with Lancaster County, Pennsylvania, quiltmakers for many years. It is a familiar and favorite pattern of the staff and shoppers at The Old Country Store, which specializes in fabrics and locally made quilts. People love the pattern—and many want to buy it—but the design is virtually unknown in other areas. Nor has a detailed pattern been available for quiltmakers who can't borrow it from a friend or family member.

Here, then, are patterns for making the traditional Dahlia quilt, as well as two quilt-sized Dahlia variations. We've also included smaller projects using the Dahlia pattern that can be finished within a day or two.

This design presents challenges in its piecing. To establish our Dahlia pattern we used the expertise available within our own neighborhood. Lancaster County has hundreds of quilters, and we visited a few whom we know are competent makers of Dahlia quilts. We stood at the elbows of several women to watch them make a Dahlia patch. Each went about it in a slightly different way. Each ended with a beautiful finished block. Each assured us that it really isn't difficult. We came home inspired and successfully completed our own Dahlia.

We have attempted to make the instructions clear and precise. We give the sequence in steps and provide illustrations for additional clarity. We hope that your own Dahlia quilts and projects will be a source of joy, both in their making and using.

Traditional Dahlia *(pattern begins on page 7)*

(top) Dahlia and Tulip Quilt *(pattern begins on page 23)*;
(bottom) Dahlia with Quilted Block Quilt *(pattern begins on page 41)*

Traditional Dahlia Quilt

Finished size is approximately 95" x 112"

Fabric Requirements

Fabric 1—Templates 4, 5, Cone A—
  4³/₄ yds. total

Fabric 2—Templates 1, 3, 7, Cone B, C—
  5⁷/₈ yds. total

Fabric 3—Template 8 (Sashing Strips)—
  2¹/₈ yds.

Fabric 4—Templates 2, 6—1³/₄ yds.

Fabric 5—Backing—fabric to measure
  98" x 116"

Binding—1¹/₂ yds.

Batting—98" x 116"

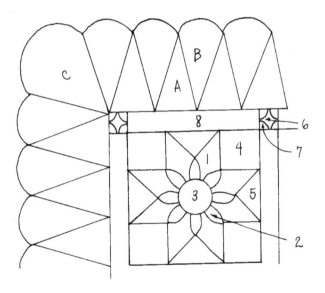

Making the Dahlia Patches

  The Traditional Dahlia patch is made up of five shapes which will be identified in the text as follows:

1. Tree (Template 1 on page 12)—
   cut 160 of Fabric 2
2. Petal (Template 2 on page 14)—
   cut 160 of Fabric 4
3. Circle (Template 3 on page 13)—
   cut 20 of Fabric 2
4. Square (Template 4 on page 13)—
   cut 80 of Fabric 1
5. Triangle (Template 5 on page 14)—
   cut 40 squares of Fabric 1 and cut each diagonally to form 80 triangles

1. Make gathers along the straight edge of the petals. To do so, use a double strand of thread and a medium sized needle. Make a knot at the end of the thread. By hand, begin stitching ¹/₄" from the side edge of the petal and ¹/₄" from the straight edge of the petal.

  Make a tiny backstitch at the beginning to secure the knot so it cannot pop through the fabric when you pull the gathers. Make running stitches along the edge, using slightly less than a ¹/₄" seam allowance so the gathering stitches will be hidden in the seam line when the petals are attached to the circle later on.

  Pull stitches tightly as you go, creating puckers or gathers in the fabric.

  Stitch to ¹/₄" from the other edge of the

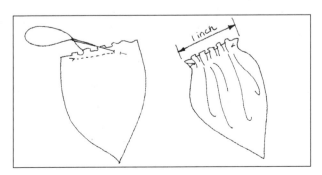

petal, making enough gathers so that the petal measures 1" along the straight edge. Make a backstitch and knot the thread to hold the gathers firmly in place. Repeat for all petals.

2. Holding the tree so the tip is down and the trunk is up, sew a gathered petal to the left side of each tree curve. Place the petal on top of the tree, right sides together. Pin the petal to the tree at both ends (A). Begin stitching at the point of the petal and stitch toward the tree trunk. Ease the fullness of the petal to fit the curve of the tree as you stitch (B).

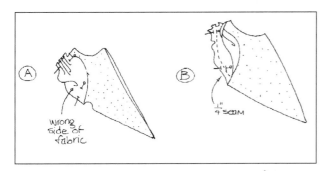

3. Pin triangles onto the right, straight sides of 80 of the trees so that the long sides of the triangles face the left sides of the trees. Begin stitching at the trunk of each tree and stitch toward the tip. Press the seam toward the tree.

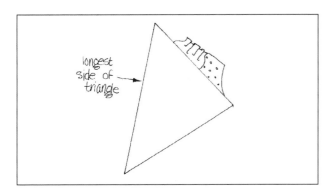

4. Sew squares to the right sides of the remaining 80 trees. Begin sewing at the trunk of each

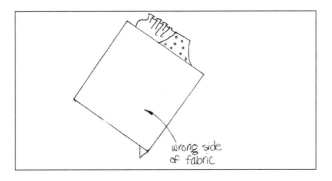

tree and stitch toward the tip. (The tip of the tree will extend slightly beyond the end of the square.) Press the seam toward the tree.

5. Stitch a petal-tree-triangle unit to a petal-tree-square unit. Pin the units together near the center where the petal point meets the tree on one unit and the square meets the tree on the other unit. Have the petal-tree junction and the tree-square junction facing in opposite directions with the seams butted up against each other. Place a pin at this point to assure that the seams meet accurately and cannot shift during stitching. Place a second pin connecting the base of the petal and the trunk of the tree.

With the petal on top, begin stitching at the trunk of the tree, easing the petal to fit the curve. Continue stitching over the pinned joint and through the end of the tree and tri-angle. Press the seam toward the tree. Continue this sequence until a square patch is completed.

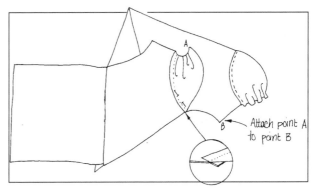

6. Fold the center circle in half and then into quarters to mark it into equal quadrants. Place a pin at each quarter point. Fit the circle into the round opening of the patch, having right sides together and fitting two petals into each quarter of the circle. Pin in place. Stitch around the circle through all thicknesses.

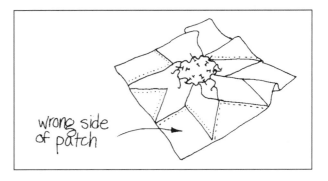

You will need a total of 20 Dahlia patches.

Making the Corner Patches

The corner blocks are made up of two templates which will be identified in the text as follows:

1. Wedge (Template 7 on page 14)—cut 120 of Fabric 2 (when marking and cutting, mark the center point on each wedge curve)
2. Window (Template 6 on page 14)—cut 30 of Fabric 4 (when marking and cutting, mark the center point of each curve)

1. With right sides together, lay one window on top of one wedge piece, having the point of the window even with the point of the wedge. Stitch, easing the window curve to fit the curve of the wedge, matching the center points on each piece.

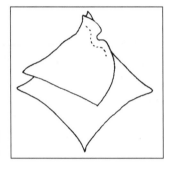

2. Attach a second wedge to the wedge/window unit, again laying the window on top of the wedge and easing the pieces to match. Continue with a third and fourth wedge until the square block is completed. Press seams toward center.

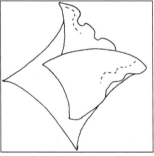

Adding the Sashing

When you have finished the corner blocks, you are ready to cut sashing strips. Sashing strips should be cut the exact width of the corner blocks (approximately 3½") by the exact width of the Dahlia patch (approximately 15"). Cut 49 strips.

1. Sew a sashing strip to the *top only* of 16 Dahlia patches.

2. Sew a sashing strip to the *top* and *bottom* of the four remaining patches.

3. Join the patches, making four rows of five patches each. (Be sure that the patch with sashing attached to the bottom is the last patch attached to each of the four rows.)

4. Stitch a corner block to one end of 20 sashing strips.

5. Stitch a corner block to *both* ends of each of the remaining five sashing strips.

6. Join the sashing units together to form five long strips. (Be sure that the sashing unit with a corner block attached to *both* ends is at the bottom of each of the five lengths.)

7. Sew the sashing strips to the rows of patches until all the patches are joined.

Making a Cone Border

The cone border is made up of three templates identified in the text as follows:

1. Cone A (Template on page 17)—cut 58 of Fabric 1
2. Cone B (Template on page 16)—cut 62 of Fabric 2
3. Cone C (Template on page 15)—cut 4 of Fabric 2

1. With right sides together, stitch Cone A to Cone B with the narrow points of the cones opposite each 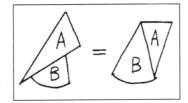 other. (The point of each cone will extend beyond the bottom of the cone to which it is attached.)

Continue this sequence to form two rows of cones, with 13 of Cone A and 14 of Cone B on each row.

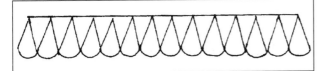

2. Attach the straight edge of one cone border to the top of the quilt top and the straight edge of the other cone border to the bottom of the quilt top, so that the point of Cone B is even with the corner of the quilt on each end.

3. Repeat the sequence for the side borders, having 16 of Cone A and 17 of Cone B on each row. Attach the borders to each side so that the point of Cone B is even with the corner of the quilt on each end.

4. Use Cone C to fill in the border on each of the four corners. Begin stitching at the curved end of the cone and stitch toward the point.

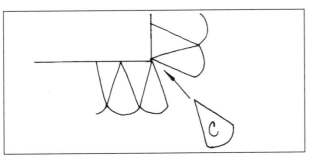

Marking Quilting Lines

Traditionally, most of the quilting on the Dahlia quilt is done as outline quilting around the pieced block. Use the quilting templates on pages 18-22 to fill in the sashing, corner blocks, and triangles around the Dahlia.

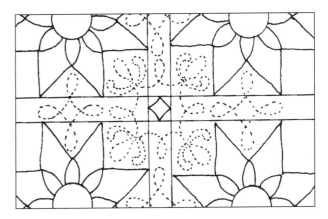

To quilt along seam lines, simply follow the line of the pieced seam. (No marking is necessary.) To mark the quilting lines for the sashing, use a very light pencil line or mark with a quilt marking tool available in quilt and fabric shops. Remember that quilting lines are not covered by quilting stitches, so the lines should be light or removable.

Quilting

You will need a backing fabric measuring 98" x 116," and batting of the same size.

Layer the backing, batting, and Dahlia top in a quilting frame, or baste the layers together securely so the layers will not shift if you will be using a small hoop.

The quilting stitch is a simple running stitch that pierces through all three layers of the quilt and holds them together. Quilting also creates a decorative pattern on the quilt and adds dimension to the pieced design.

Quilting is done with a single strand of quilting thread. Knot the thread and insert the needle through the top layer of the quilt, about one inch away from where the first quilting stitch will emerge on a marked line or along a seam line. Tug the knot gently through the top layer so it is hidden between the layers. Reinsert the needle into the fabric, going through all the layers. Quilting is a rocking

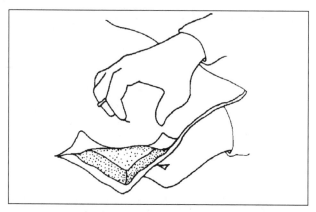

motion, with the needle going up and down as it enters and exits the layers of the quilt.

When you have used an entire length of thread, make a small knot and again pop it through the top layer of fabric, burying it in the layers of the quilt.

The goal in quilting is to have small, even stitches that are equal in length on the top and bottom of the quilt. This is best achieved with hours of practice!

Binding

1. Before binding, baste the raw edges of the quilt together around the entire circumference of the quilt. Trim away excess batting and backing.

2. Cut 2¼"-wide bias binding to measure about 520 inches in length. Fold the binding in half lengthwise, wrong sides together, and press.

3. Lay the binding strip along the scalloped edge of the quilt top, with the raw edges even and the fold of the binding facing the center of the quilt. Stitch the binding in place through all thicknesses using a ¼" seam allowance. Ease the binding around the curves, pivoting at the inside point of each scallop.

4. Fold the binding around to the back of the quilt, encasing all raw edges. Slip-stitch by hand, with the fold of the binding along the seam line.

Templates for Traditional Dahlia Quilt

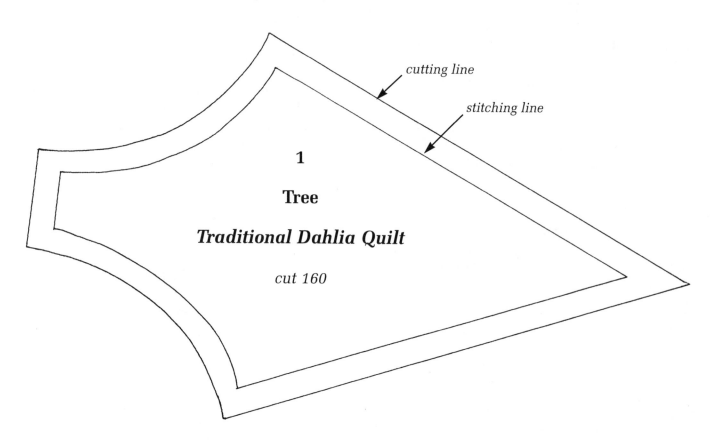

cutting line

stitching line

1

Tree

Traditional Dahlia Quilt

cut 160

Templates for Traditional Dahlia Quilt

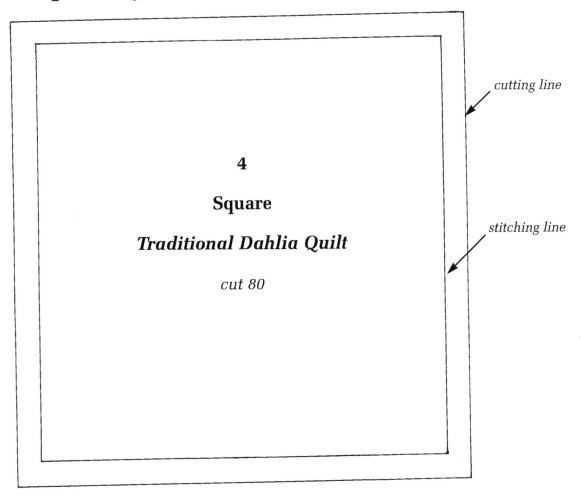

cutting line

4

Square

Traditional Dahlia Quilt

cut 80

stitching line

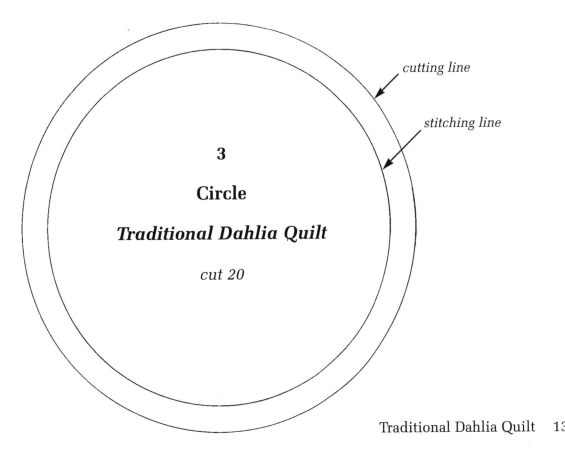

cutting line

stitching line

3

Circle

Traditional Dahlia Quilt

cut 20

Templates for Traditional Dahlia Quilt

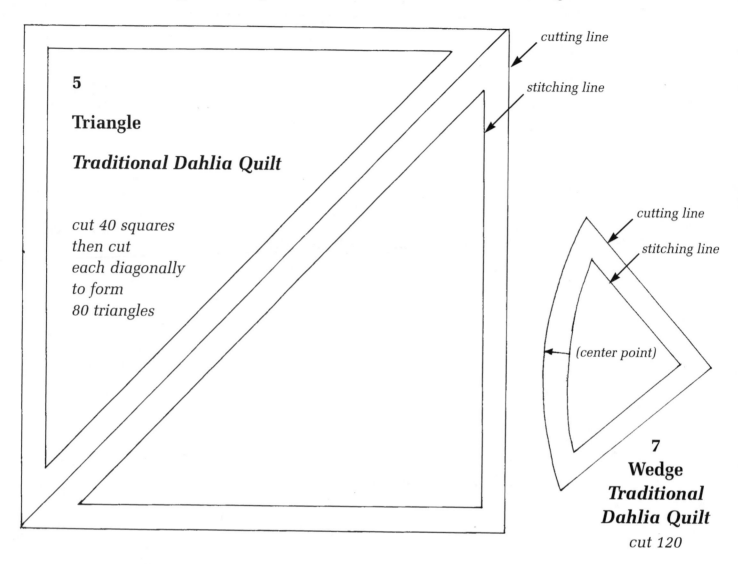

cutting line

stitching line

5

Triangle

Traditional Dahlia Quilt

*cut 40 squares
then cut
each diagonally
to form
80 triangles*

cutting line

stitching line

(center point)

7
Wedge
*Traditional
Dahlia Quilt*

cut 120

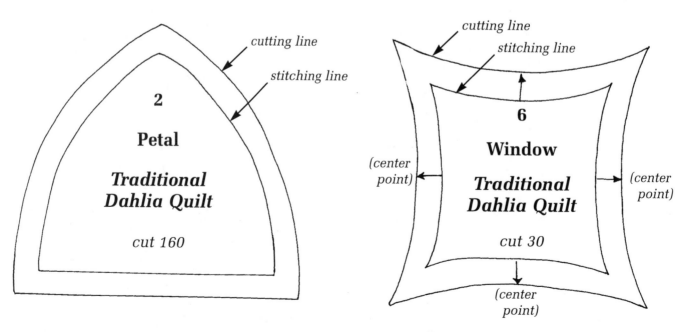

cutting line

stitching line

2

Petal

*Traditional
Dahlia Quilt*

cut 160

cutting line

stitching line

6

Window

*Traditional
Dahlia Quilt*

cut 30

*(center
point)*

*(center
point)*

*(center
point)*

Templates for Cone Border, Traditional Dahlia Quilt

cutting line

stitching line

Cone Border C

Traditional Dahlia Quilt

cut 4

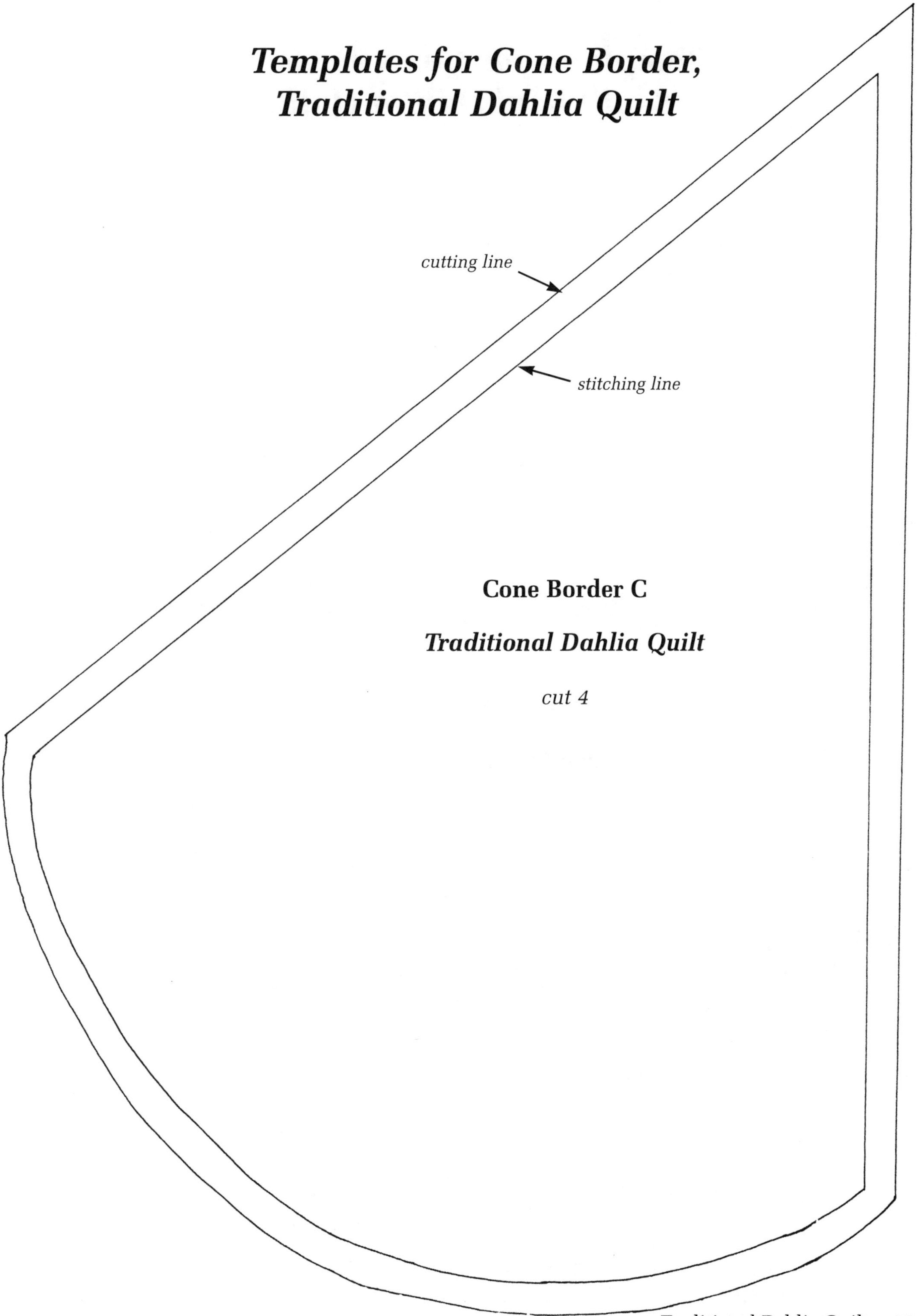

Templates for Cone Border, Traditional Dahlia Quilt

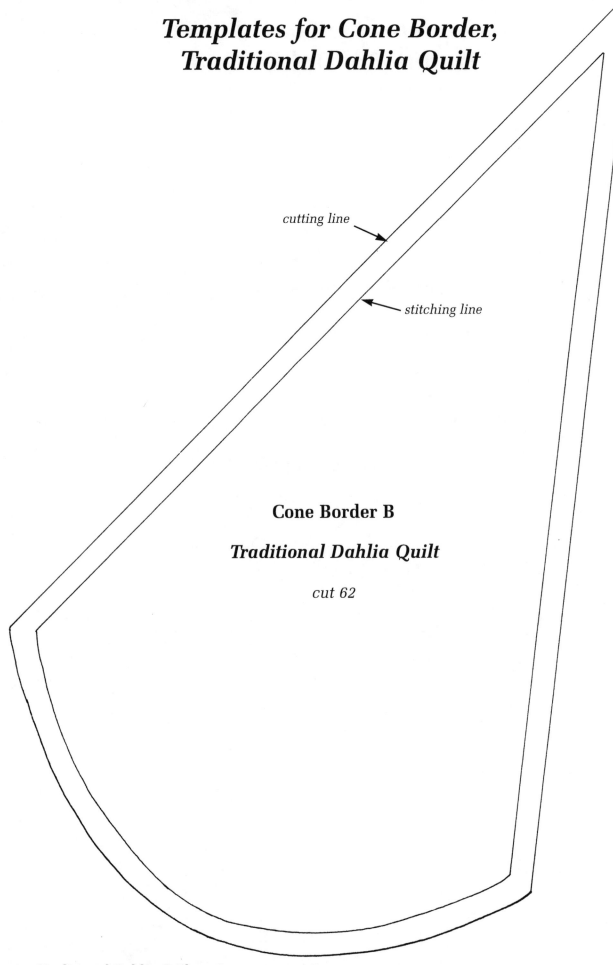

cutting line

stitching line

Cone Border B

Traditional Dahlia Quilt

cut 62

Templates for Cone Border, Traditional Dahlia Quilt

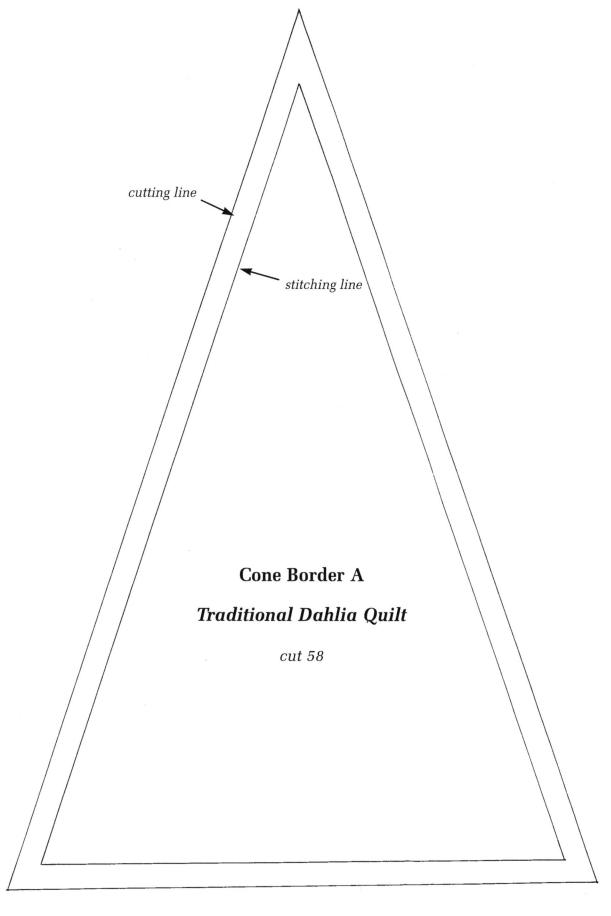

cutting line

stitching line

Cone Border A

Traditional Dahlia Quilt

cut 58

Quilting Template for Traditional Dahlia Quilt

Quilting Template for Traditional Dahlia Quilt

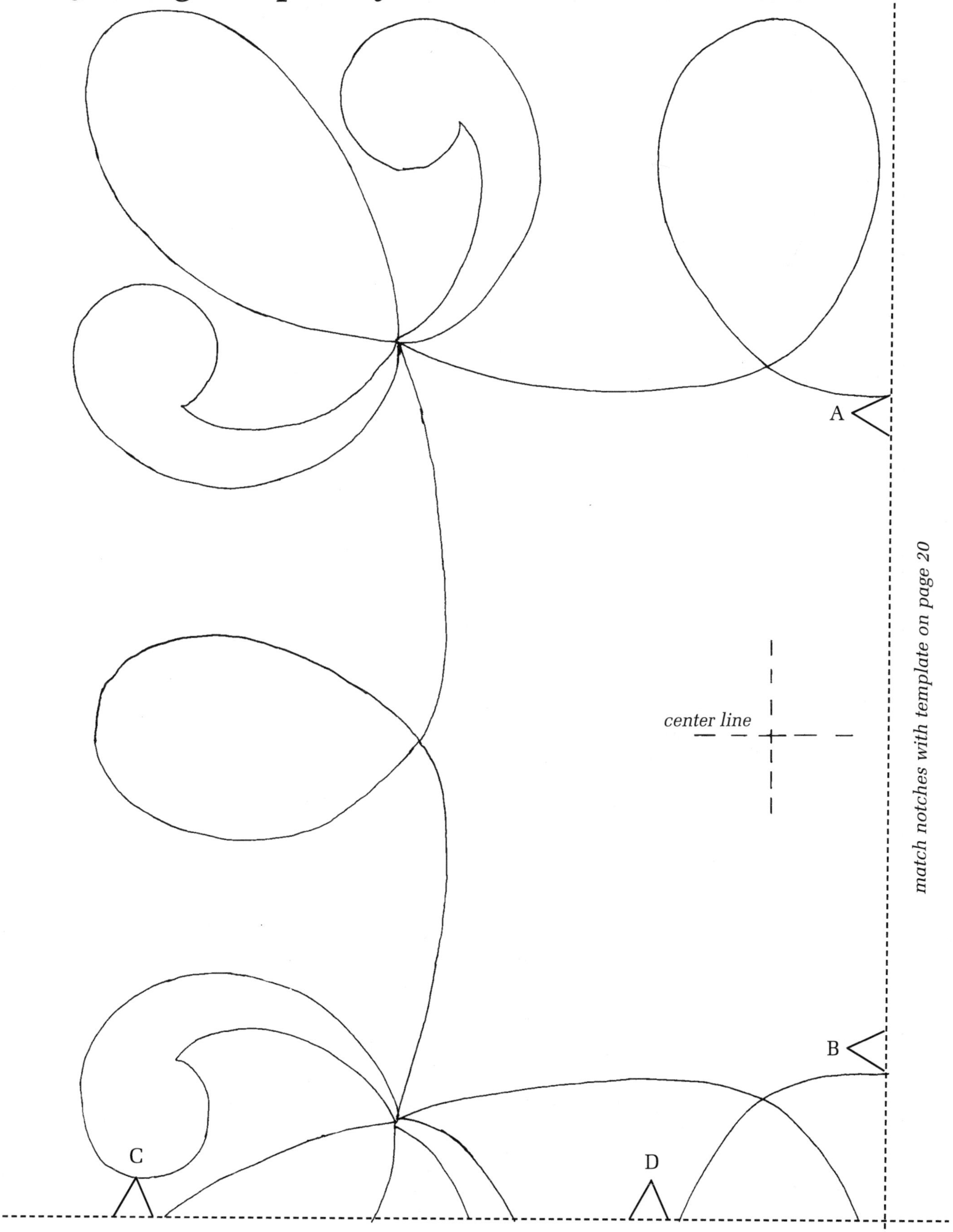

A

B

C

D

center line

match notches with template on page 20

match notches with template on page 21

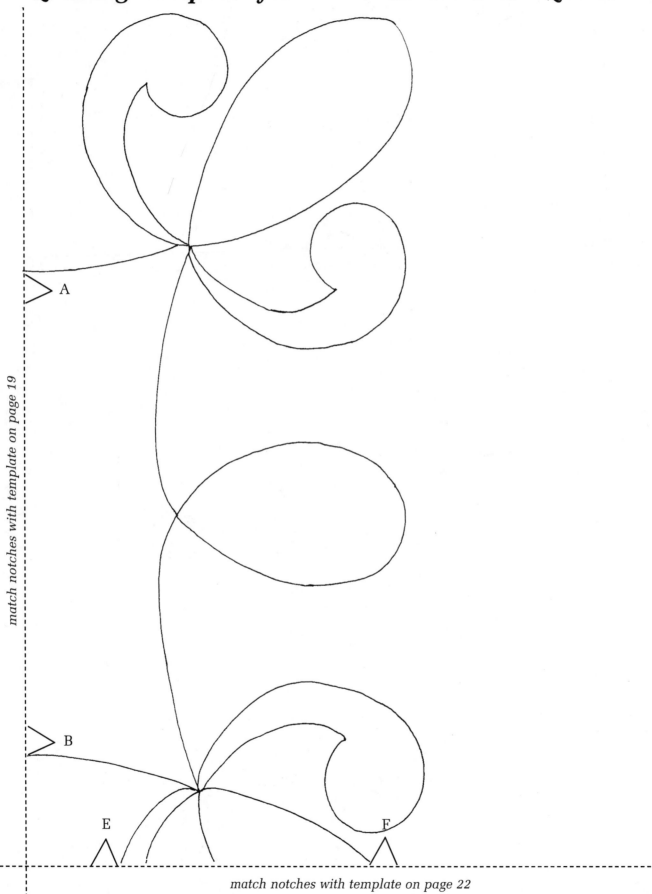

match notches with template on page 19

A

B

E

F

match notches with template on page 22

Quilting Template for Traditional Dahlia Quilt

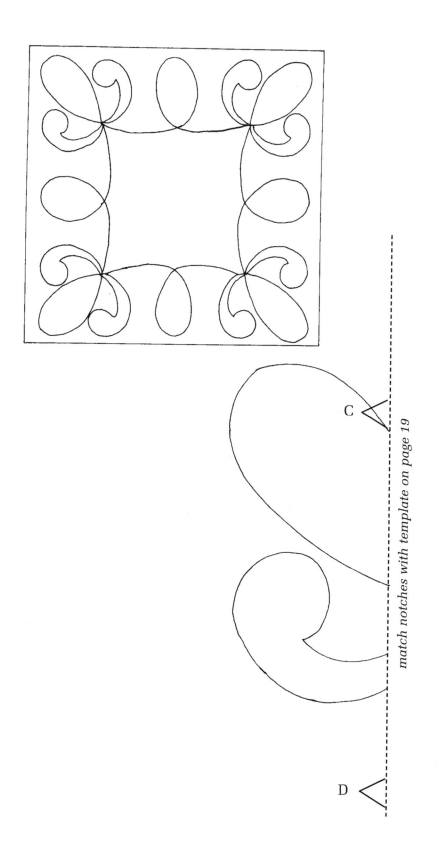

C

D

match notches with template on page 19

Quilting Template for Traditional Dahlia Quilt

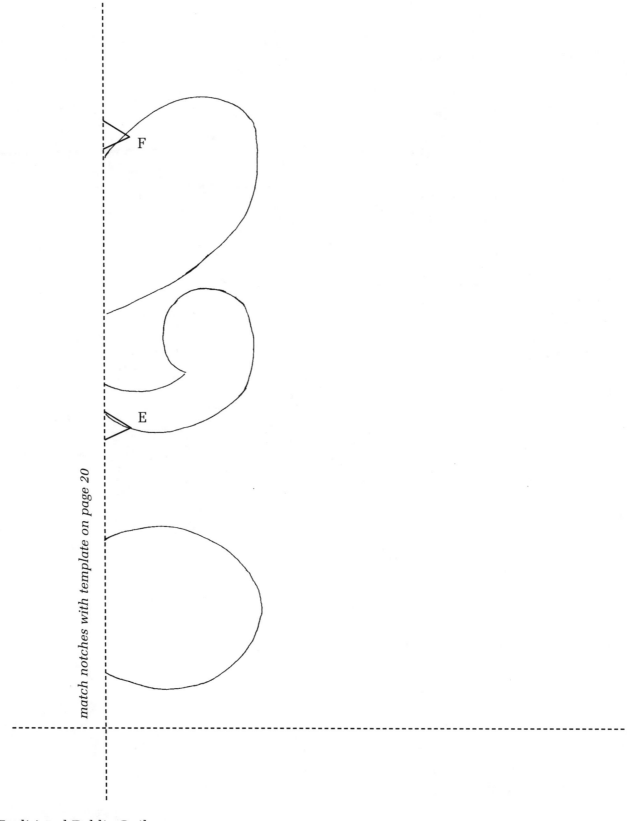

F

E

match notches with template on page 20

Dahlia and Tulip Quilt

Finished size is approximately 90" x 105"

The Dahlia and Tulip Quilt uses the Traditional Dahlia pattern but adds a pieced tulip in each corner of the patch in place of the plain square. Instead of sashing between the blocks, tulips create a floral quartet between each Dahlia.

You will need a total of 20 Dahlia patches and 80 pieced tulips to complete the design.

Fabric Requirements

Fabric 1—Templates 4, 6, 9, E, F—4³/₄ yds.
Fabric 2—Templates 7, 10, D—4¹/₄ yds.
Fabric 3—Templates 2, 8—2¹/₄ yds.
Fabric 4—Templates 3, 5—⁷/₈ yd.
Fabric 5—Template 1—³/₄ yd.
Fabric 6—Inner border—2¹/₂ yds.*
Fabric 7—Backing—Fabric to measure 95" x 110")
Binding—1 yd. (*If binding is the same as the inner border, no additional fabric is needed for the binding.)
Batting—95" x 110"

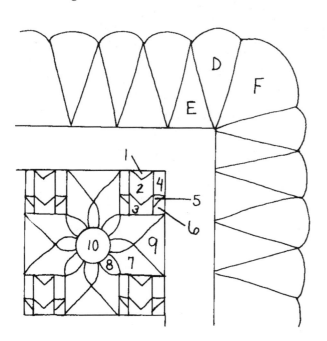

Making the Tulip Squares

The Tulip Square is built as a series of four vertical units which are joined to make the square patch. The templates are numbered 1 through 6 and should be cut as follows:

Template 1 (page 30)—from Fabric 5, cut 160 pieces, 80 facing in one direction; 80 facing in the opposite direction

Template 2 (page 30)—from Fabric 3, cut 160 pieces, 80 facing in one direction; 80 facing in the opposite direction

Template 3 (page 30)—from Fabric 4, cut 160 pieces, 80 facing in one direction; 80 facing in the opposite direction

Template 4 (page 30)—cut 160 from Fabric 1

Template 5 (page 30)—cut 80 squares from Fabric 4 and cut each square in half diagonally to form 160 triangles

Template 6 (page 30)—from Fabric 1, cut 160 pieces, 80 facing in one direction; 80 facing in the opposite direction

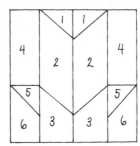

1. Sew Template 1 to Template 2.

2. Sew the 1,2 unit to Template 3.

3. Sew Template 5 to Template 6.

4. Sew the 5,6 unit to Template 4.

5. Sew the 1,2,3 unit to the 4,5,6 unit.

6. Repeat steps 1 through 5, using the pieces cut in the opposite direction.

7. Sew the two halves of the tulip patch together.

24   Dahlia and Tulip Quilt

Making the Dahlia Patches

The Traditional Dahlia patch is made up of five shapes which will be identified in the text as follows:

1. Tree (Template 7 on page 31)—
   cut 160 of Fabric 2
2. Petal (Template 8 on page 31)—
   cut 160 of Fabric 3
3. Circle (Template 10 on page 31)—
   cut 20 of Fabric 2
4. Triangle (Template 9 on page 29)—
   cut 40 squares of Fabric 1 and cut each diagonally to form 80 triangles

1. Make gathers along the straight edge of the petals. To do so, use a double strand of thread and a medium sized needle. Make a knot at the end of the thread. By hand, begin stitching ¼" from the side edge of the petal and ¼" from the straight edge of the petal.

Make a tiny backstitch at the beginning to secure the knot so it cannot pop through the fabric when you pull the gathers. Make running stitches along the edge, using slightly less than a ¼" seam allowance so the gathering stitches will be hidden in the seam line when the petals are attached to the circle later on.

Pull stitches tightly as you go, creating puckers or gathers in the fabric.

Stitch to ¼" from the other edge of the petal, making enough gathers so that the petal measures 1" along the straight edge. Make a backstitch and knot the thread to hold the gathers firmly in place. Repeat for all petals.

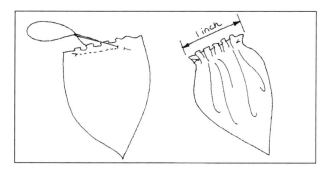

2. Holding the tree so the tip is down and the trunk is up, sew a gathered petal to the left side of each tree curve. Place the petal on top of the tree, right sides together. Pin the petal to the tree at both ends (A). Begin stitching at the point of the petal and stitch toward the tree trunk. Ease the fullness of the petal to fit the curve of the tree as you stitch (B).

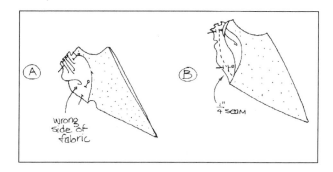

3. Pin triangles onto the right, straight sides of 80 of the trees so that the long sides of the triangles face the left sides of the trees. Begin stitching at the trunk of each tree and stitch toward the tip. Press the seam toward the tree.

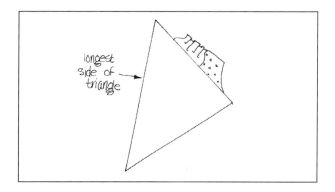

4. Sew tulip squares to the right sides of the remaining trees. Begin sewing at the trunk of the tree and stitch toward the tip (The tip of the tree will extend slightly beyond the end of the square.) Press the seam toward the tree.

The top of the tulip square should always be pointing toward the top of the quilt.

Be sure to place the *leaf end* of the tulip against the trunk end on half the Dahlia trees and against the *pointed end* on the other half of the Dahlia trees. Be alert to the position of

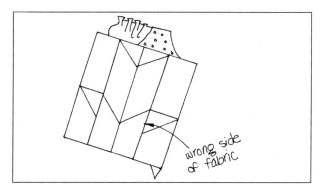

the tulip when assembling the patches so that all tulips are sitting upright.

5. Stitch a petal-tree-triangle unit to a petal-tree-tulip unit. Pin the units together near the center where the petal point meets the tree on one unit and the tulip patch meets the tree on the other unit. Have the petal-tree junction and the tree-tulip junction facing in opposite directions with the seams butted up against each other. Place a pin at this point to assure that the seams meet accurately and cannot shift during stitching. Place a second pin connecting the base of the petal and the trunk of the tree.

With the petal on top, begin stitching at the trunk of the tree, easing the petal to fit the curve. Continue stitching over the pinned joint and through the end of the tree and triangle. Press the seam toward the tree. Continue this sequence until a square patch is completed.

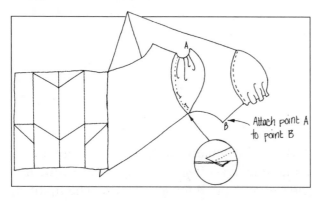

Attach point A to point B

6. Fold the center circle in half and then into quarters to mark it into equal quadrants. Place a pin at each quarter point. Fit the circle into the round opening of the patch, having right sides together and fitting two petals into each quarter of the circle. Pin in place. Stitch around the circle through all thicknesses.

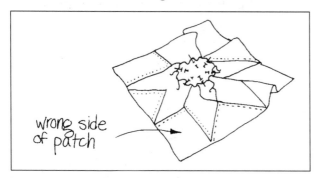

wrong side of patch

Assembling the Dahlia and Tulip Patches

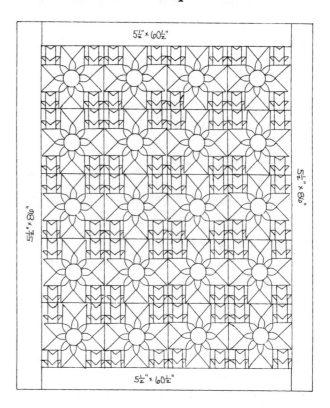

$5\frac{1}{2}" \times 60\frac{1}{2}"$

$5\frac{1}{2}" \times 86"$

$5\frac{1}{2}" \times 86"$

$5\frac{1}{2}" \times 60\frac{1}{2}"$

1. Join the patches vertically, making four strips of five blocks each.

2. Sew the vertical rows together until all the blocks are joined.

3. Cut two borders, each measuring $5\frac{1}{2}"$ wide x $60\frac{1}{2}"$ long. (Note: Measure the bottom and top width of the joined patches and adjust the $60\frac{1}{2}"$ measurement if necessary to fit your individual quilt.)

4. Sew the borders to the top and bottom of the quilt.

5. Cut two borders, each measuring $5\frac{1}{2}"$ wide x 86" long. (Note: Measure the length of the joined patches and adjust the 86" measurement if necessary to fit your individual quilt.)

6. Sew the borders to the sides of the quilt.

Making a Cone Border

The cone border is made up of three templates identified in the text as follows:

1. Cone D (Template on page 32)—cut 66 of Fabric 5
2. Cone E (Template on page 33)—cut 62 of Fabric 1
3. Cone F (Template on page 34-35)—cut 4 of Fabric 1

1. With right sides together, stitch Cone D to Cone E with the narrow points of the cones opposite each other. (The point of 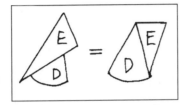 each cone will extend beyond the bottom of the cone to which it is attached.)

Continue this sequence to form two rows of cones, with 15 of Cone D and 14 of Cone E on each row.

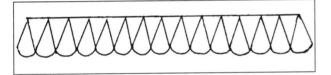

2. Attach the straight edge of one cone border to the top of the quilt top and the straight edge of the other cone border to the bottom of the quilt top, so that the point of Cone D is even with the corner of the quilt on each end.

3. Repeat the sequence for the side borders, having 18 of Cone D and 17 of Cone E on each row. Attach the borders to each side so that the point of Cone D is even with the corner of the quilt on each end.

4. Use Cone F to fill in the border on each of the four corners. Begin stitching at the curved end of the cone and stitch toward the point.

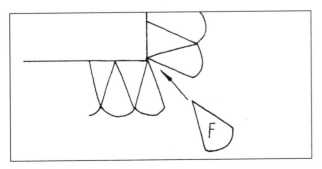

Marking Quilting Lines

Most of the quilting on the Dahlia and Tulip Quilt outlines the pieced design and does not need to be marked. Quilting around the pieced tulip, dahlia, and cone accentuates and enhances the pieced design and gives dimension to the quilt. Use the quilting design given on pages 36-38 to decorate the inner border.

Transfer the quilting lines onto the inner border using very light or removable markings. Transferring the design onto the fabric can be done by laying the design under the fabric and tracing it.

If the fabric is dark and difficult to see through, the design will have to be transferred another way. One option is to trace over the quilting lines with soft chalk. Lay it face down on the fabric and rub gently to rub the chalk marks onto the fabric.

Another possibility is to make your own template from cardboard or plastic with narrow slits cut out on the marked lines. Using a sharp pencil and very gentle pressure, trace the lines onto the fabric.

Quilting

You will need a backing fabric measuring at least 95" x 110," and batting of the same size.

Layer the backing, batting, and Dahlia top in a quilting frame, or baste the layers together securely so the layers will not shift if you will be using a small hoop.

The quilting stitch is a simple running stitch that pierces through all three layers of the quilt and holds them together. Quilting also creates a decorative pattern on the quilt

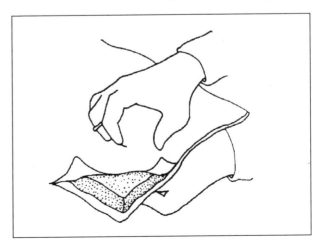

and adds dimension to the pieced design.

Quilting is done with a single strand of quilting thread. Knot the thread and insert the needle through the top layer of the quilt, about one inch away from where the first quilting stitch will emerge on a marked line or along a seam line. Tug the knot gently through the top layer so it is hidden between the layers. Reinsert the needle into the fabric, going through all the layers. Quilting is a rocking motion, with the needle going up and down as it enters and exits the layers of the quilt.

When you have used an entire length of thread, make a small knot and again pop it through the top layer of fabric, burying it in the layers of the quilt.

The goal in quilting is to have small, even stitches that are equal in length on the top and bottom of the quilt. This is best achieved with hours of practice!

Binding

1. Before binding, baste the raw edges of the quilt together around the entire circumference of the quilt. Trim away excess batting and backing.

2. Cut $2\frac{1}{4}$"-wide bias binding to measure about 500 inches in length. Fold the binding in half lengthwise, wrong sides together, and press.

3. Lay the binding strip along the scalloped edge of the quilt top, with the raw edges even and the fold of the binding facing the center of the quilt. Stitch the binding in place through all thicknesses using a $\frac{1}{4}$" seam allowance. Ease the binding around the curves, pivoting at the inside point of each scallop.

4. Fold the binding around to the back of the quilt, encasing all raw edges. Slip-stitch by hand, with the fold of the binding along the seam line.

Dahlia Template for Dahlia and Tulip Quilt

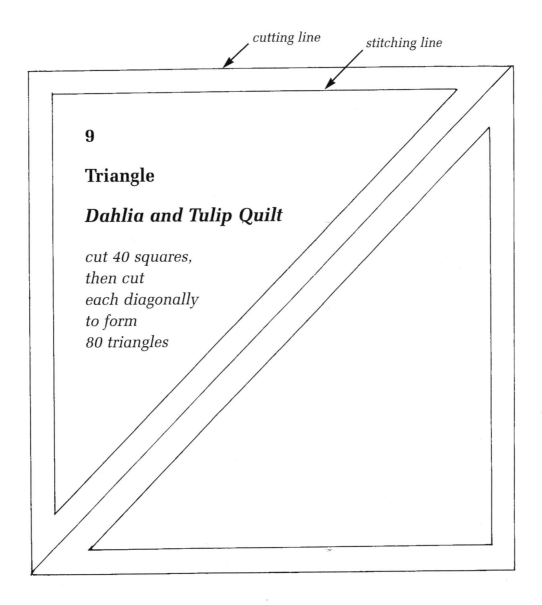

cutting line   stitching line

9

Triangle

Dahlia and Tulip Quilt

*cut 40 squares,
then cut
each diagonally
to form
80 triangles*

Tulip Templates for Dahlia and Tulip Quilt

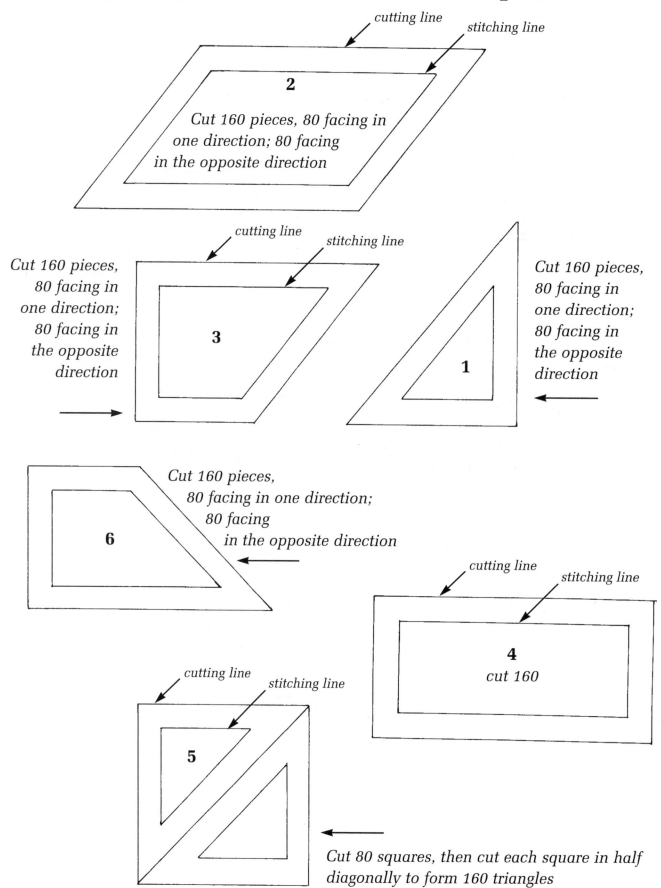

cutting line

stitching line

2

Cut 160 pieces, 80 facing in one direction; 80 facing in the opposite direction

cutting line

stitching line

Cut 160 pieces, 80 facing in one direction; 80 facing in the opposite direction

3

Cut 160 pieces, 80 facing in one direction; 80 facing in the opposite direction

1

Cut 160 pieces, 80 facing in one direction; 80 facing in the opposite direction

6

cutting line

stitching line

4

cut 160

cutting line

stitching line

5

Cut 80 squares, then cut each square in half diagonally to form 160 triangles

Dahlia Templates for Dahlia and Tulip Quilt

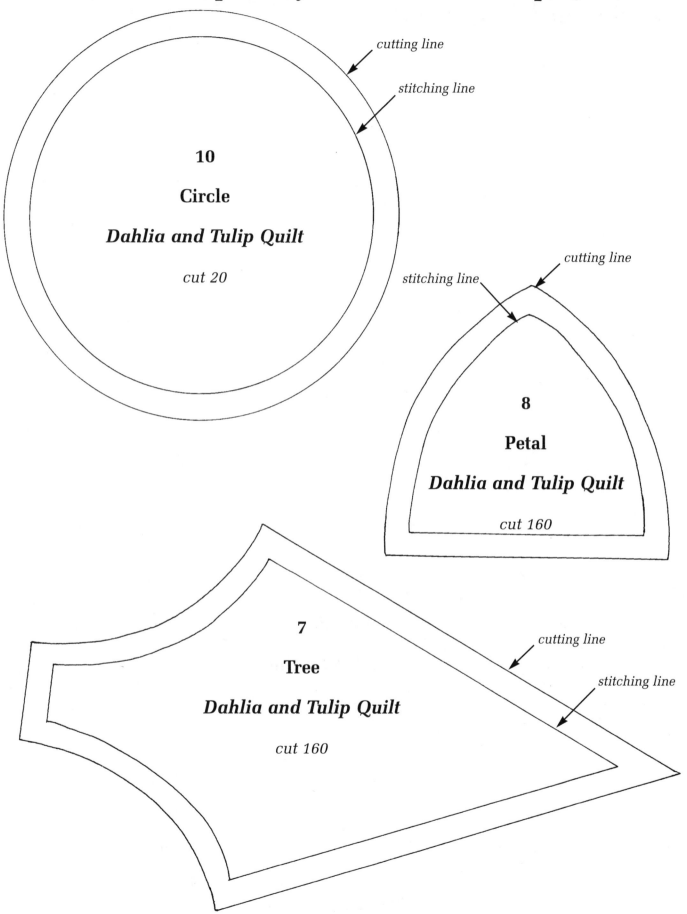

cutting line

stitching line

10

Circle

Dahlia and Tulip Quilt

cut 20

cutting line

stitching line

8

Petal

Dahlia and Tulip Quilt

cut 160

cutting line

stitching line

7

Tree

Dahlia and Tulip Quilt

cut 160

Template for Cone Border, Dahlia and Tulip Quilt

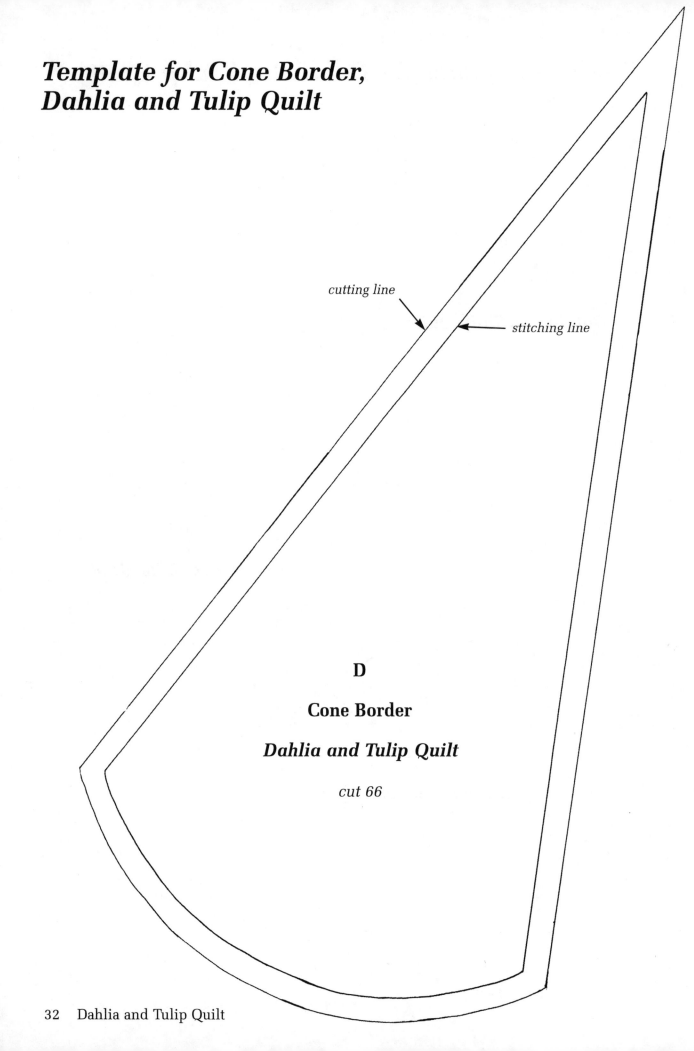

cutting line

stitching line

D

Cone Border

Dahlia and Tulip Quilt

cut 66

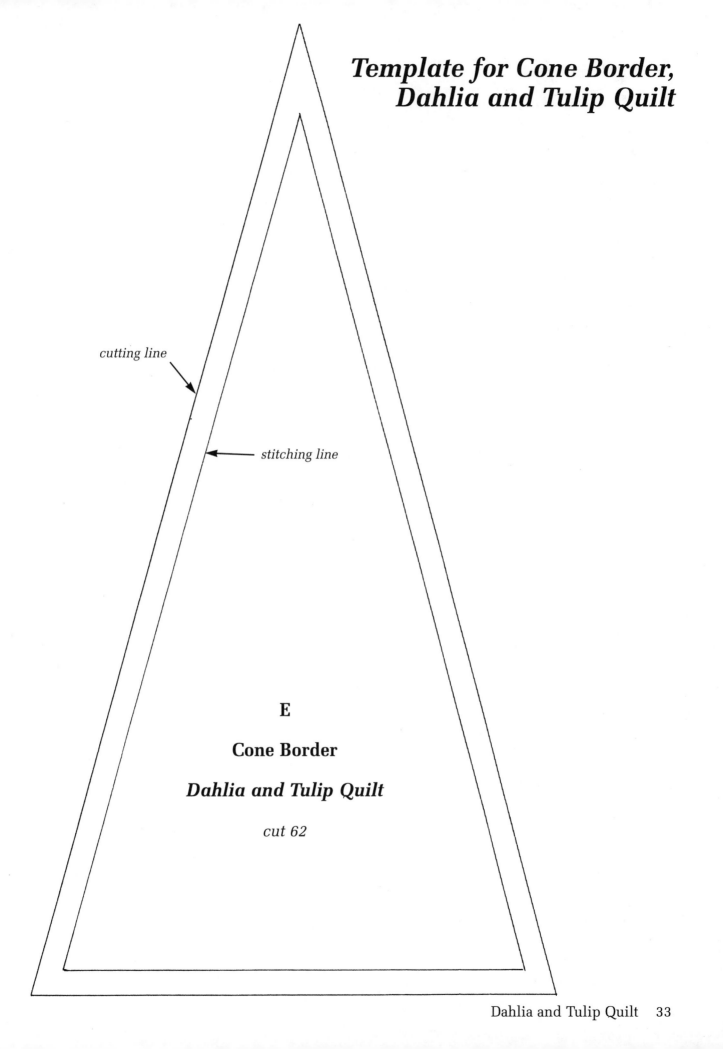

cutting line

stitching line

E

Cone Border

Dahlia and Tulip Quilt

cut 62

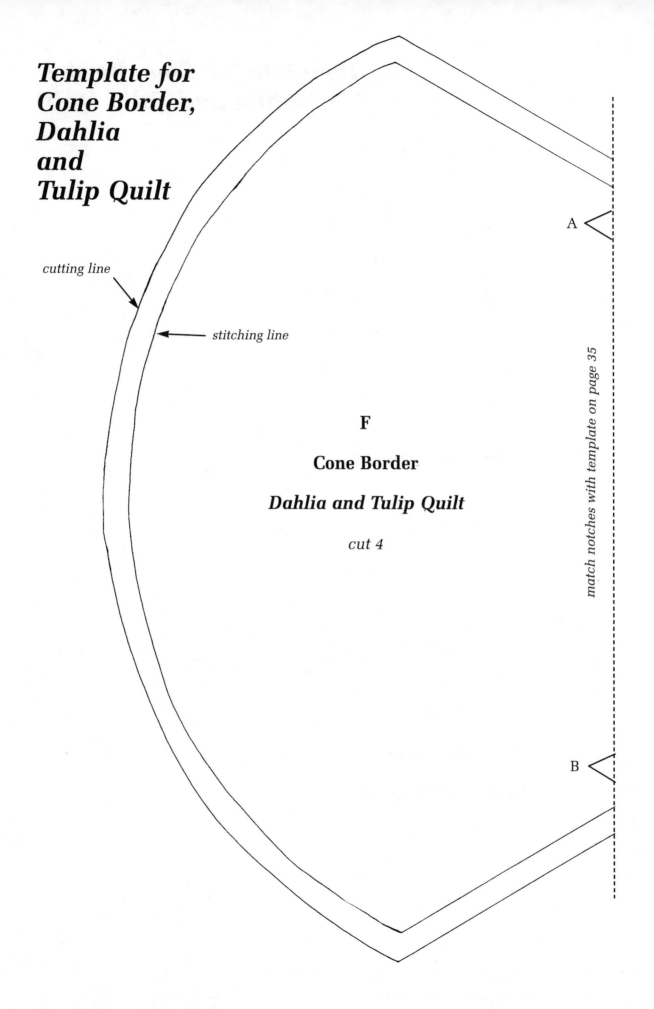

Template for Cone Border, Dahlia and Tulip Quilt

cutting line

stitching line

A

match notches with template on page 35

F

Cone Border

Dahlia and Tulip Quilt

cut 4

B

Template for Cone Border, Dahlia and Tulip Quilt

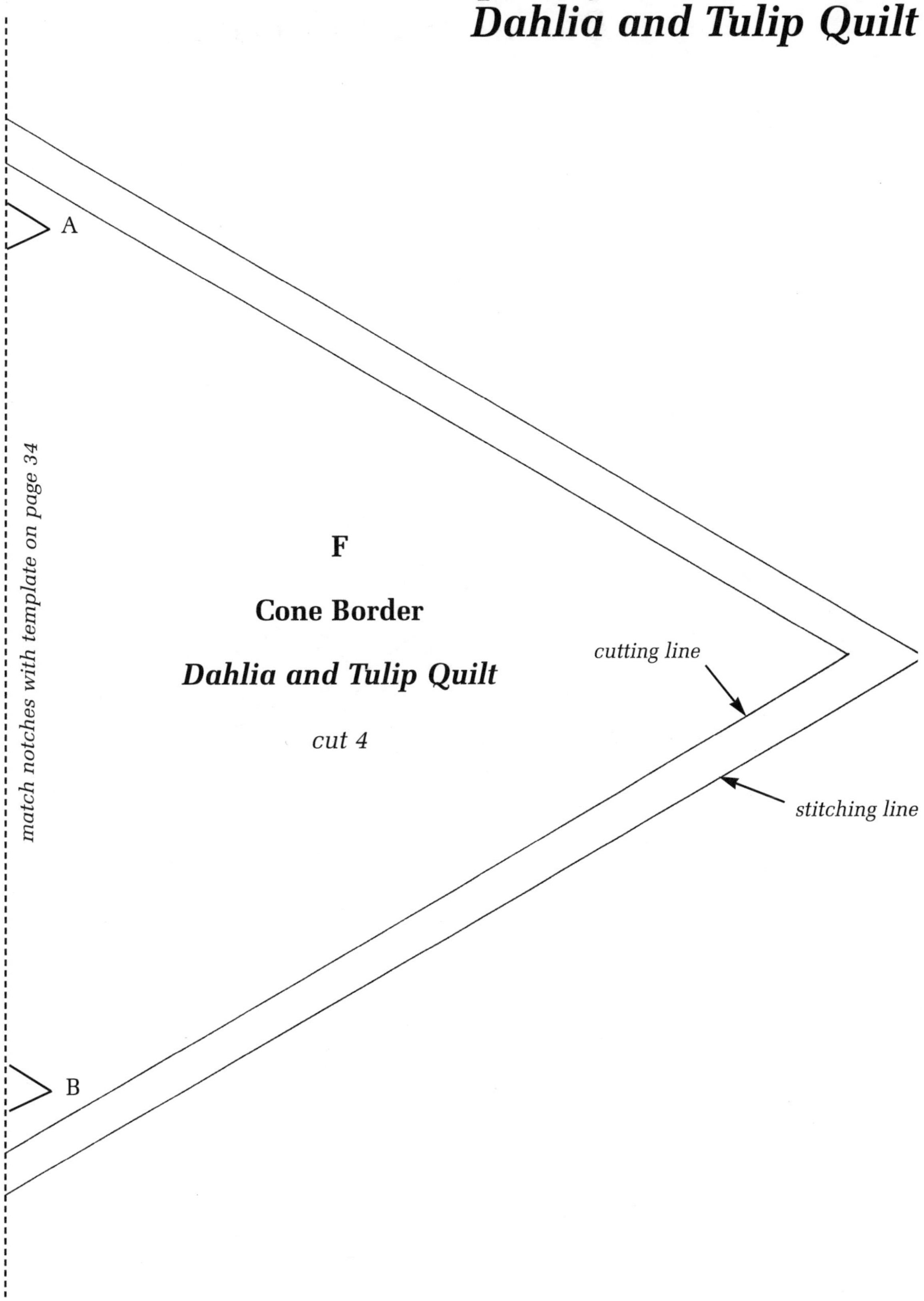
match notches with template on page 34
A
B
F
Cone Border
Dahlia and Tulip Quilt
cut 4
cutting line
stitching line

Quilting Template for Inner Border, Dahlia and Tulip Quilt

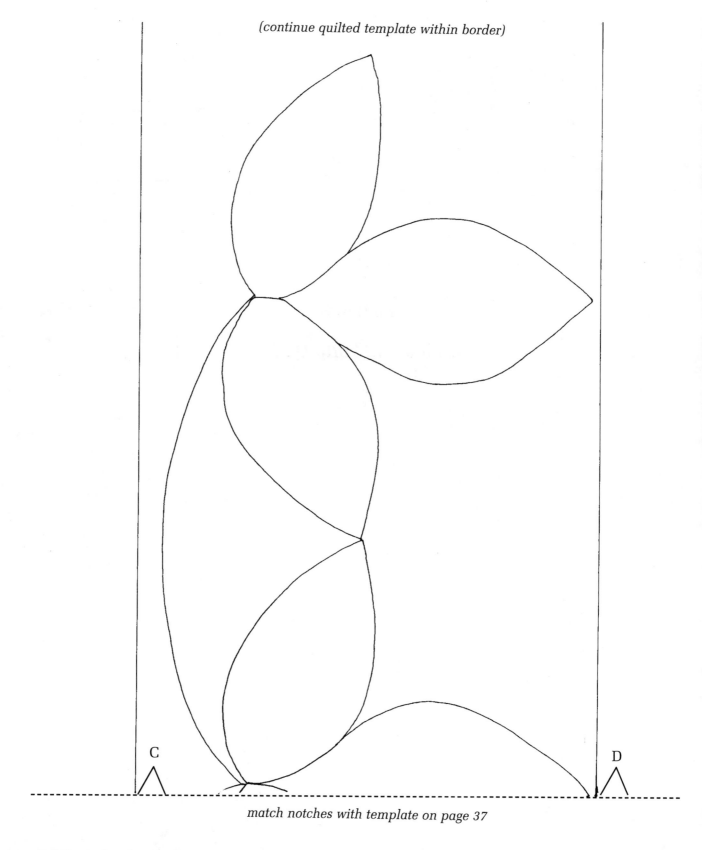

(continue quilted template within border)

C

D

match notches with template on page 37

Quilting Template for Inner Border, Dahlia and Tulip Quilt

E

match notches with template on page 38

F

D

C

match notches with template on page 36

Quilting Template for Inner Border, Dahlia and Tulip Quilt

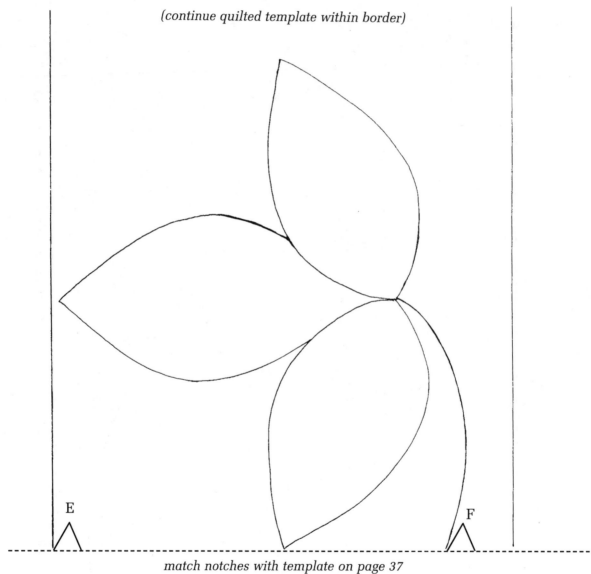

(continue quilted template within border)

E

F

match notches with template on page 37

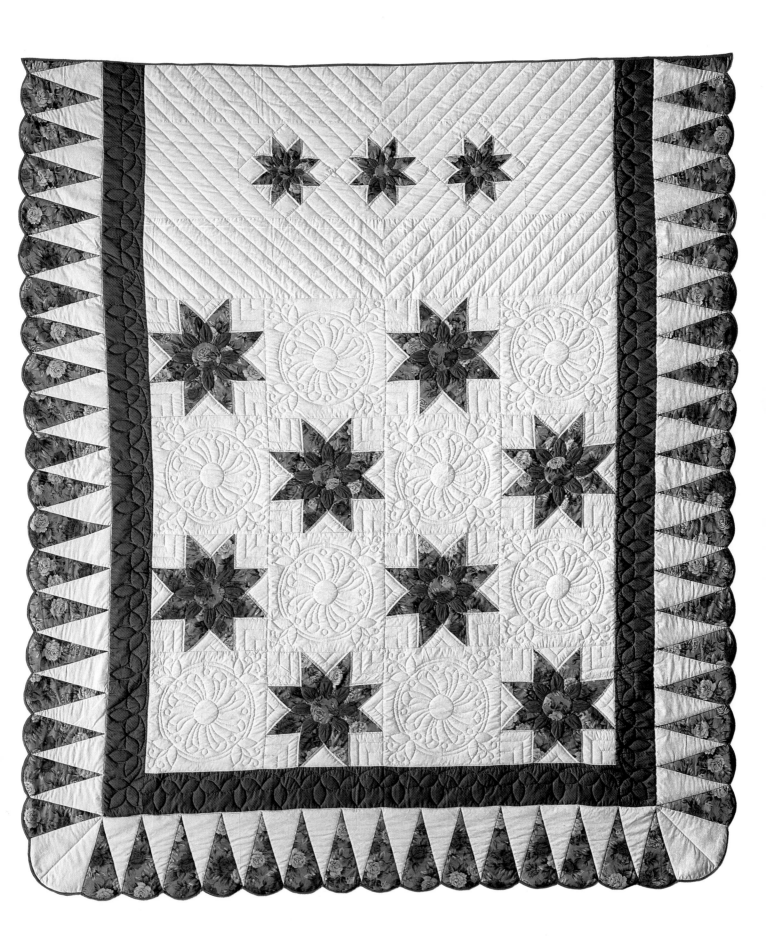

Dahlia with Quilted Block Quilt *(pattern begins on page 41)*

Dahlia Wallhanging *(pattern begins on page 57)*

Dahlia and Quilted Block Quilt

Finished size is approximately 90" x 105"

This Dahlia variation uses eight blocks of the Traditional Dahlia set against eight quilted blocks of background fabric. The pillow throw uses three patches of the Traditional Dahlia in a smaller version, tipped on their sides to make a trio of flowers covering the bed pillows.

Fabric Requirements

- **Fabric 1**—Templates 4, 5, Cone I, Cone G, J through O—5½ yds.
- **Fabric 2**—Templates 1, 3, Cone H—3⅛ yds.
- **Fabric 3**—Template 2—½ yd.
- **Fabric 4**—Inner border—2¾ yds.*
- **Fabric 5**—Backing—fabric to measure 95" x 110"
- **Binding**—1 yd. (* If binding is the same as the inner border, no additional binding fabric is needed)
- **Batting**—95" x 110"

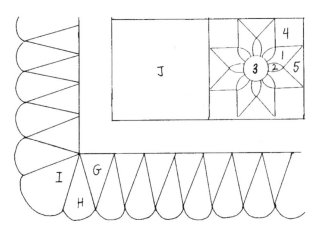

Cutting Diagram for Fabric 1

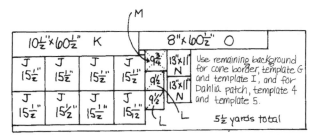

To make the most efficient use of Fabric 1, you will need to first cut the plain blocks and pillow throw sections (Letters J through O). The fabric that remains after these straight pieces have been cut out can be used for Templates 4 and 5 of the Dahlia patch and Templates I and G of the Cone Border.

- J—cut 8 patches 15½" square
- K—cut 1 rectangle 10½" x 60½"
- O—cut 1 rectangle 8" x 60½"
- N—cut 2 patches 13" x 11"
- L—cut 2 patches 9½" square, then cut each in half diagonally to form 4 triangles
- M—cut 1 patch 9¾" square, then cut diagonally into quarters to form 4 triangles

Making the Dahlia Patches

The Traditional Dahlia patch is made up of five shapes which will be identified in the text as follows:

1. Tree (Template 1 on page 50)— cut 64 of Fabric 2
2. Petal (Template 2 on page 51)— cut 64 of Fabric 3
3. Circle (Template 3 on page 48)— cut 8 of Fabric 2
4. Square (Template 4 on page 50)— cut 32 of Fabric 1
5. Triangle (Template 5 on page 51)— cut 16 squares of Fabric 1, then cut each diagonally to form 32 triangles

1. Make gathers along the straight edge of the petals. To do so, use a double strand of thread and a medium sized needle. Make a knot at the end of the thread. By hand, begin stitching ¼" from the side edge of the petal and ¼" from the straight edge of the petal.

Make a tiny backstitch at the beginning to secure the knot so it cannot pop through the fabric when you pull the gathers. Make running stitches along the edge, using slightly less than a ¼" seam allowance so the gathering stitches will be hidden in the seam line when the petals are attached to the circle later on.

Pull stitches tightly as you go, creating puckers or gathers in the fabric.

Stitch to ¼" from the other edge of the petal, making enough gathers so that the petal measures 1" along the straight edge. Make a backstitch and knot the thread to hold the gathers firmly in place. Repeat for all petals.

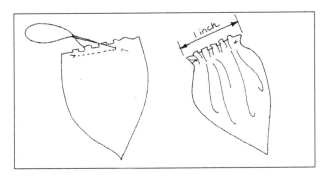

2. Holding the tree so the tip is down and the trunk is up, sew a gathered petal to the left side of each tree curve. Place the petal on top of the tree, right sides together. Pin the petal to the tree at both ends (A). Begin stitching at the point of the petal and stitch toward the tree trunk. Ease the fullness of the petal to fit the curve of the tree as you stitch (B).

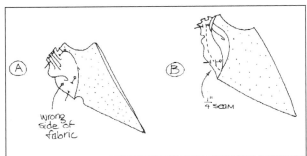

3. Pin triangles onto the right, straight sides of 32 of the trees so that the long sides of the tri-

angles face the left sides of the trees. Begin stitching at the trunk of each tree and stitch toward the tip. Press the seam toward the tree.

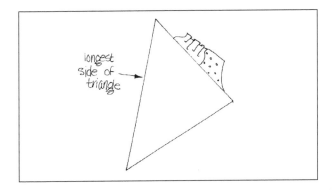

4. Sew squares to the right sides of the remaining 32 trees. Begin sewing at the trunk of each tree and stitch toward the tip. (The tip of the tree will extend slightly beyond the end of the square.) Press the seam toward the tree.

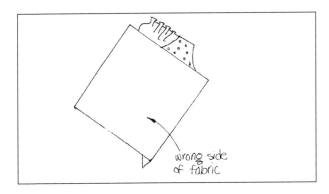

5. Stitch a petal-tree-triangle unit to a petal-tree-square unit. Pin the units together near the center where the petal point meets the tree on one unit and the square meets the tree on the other unit. Have the petal-tree junction and the tree-square junction facing in opposite directions with the seams butted up against each other. Place a pin at this point to assure that the seams meet accurately and cannot

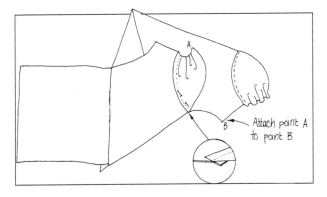

shift during stitching. Place a second pin connecting the base of the petal and the trunk of the tree.

With the petal on top, begin stitching at the trunk of the tree, easing the petal to fit the curve. Continue stitching over the pinned joint and through the end of the tree and triangle. Press the seam toward the tree. Continue this sequence until a square patch is completed.

6. Fold the center circle in half and then into quarters to mark it into equal quadrants. Place a pin at each quarter point. Fit the circle into the round opening of the patch, having right sides together and fitting two petals into each quarter of the circle. Pin in place. Stitch around the circle through all thicknesses.

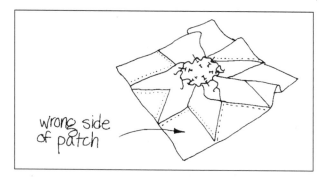

wrong side of patch

Making the Small Dahlia Patches for the Pillow Throw

Use the templates given for the Pillow Throw on page 52. You will need the following number of each template:

1. Tree (Template 1 on page 54)—cut 24 of Fabric 2
2. Petals (Template 2 on page 54)—cut 24 of Fabric 3
3. Circles (Template 3 on page 54)—cut 3 of Fabric 2
4. Squares (Template 4 on page 54)—cut 12 of Fabric 1
5. Triangles (Template 5 on page 54)—cut 12 of Fabric 1

1. Make gathers along the straight edge of the petals. To do so, use a double strand of thread and a medium sized needle. Make a knot at the end of the thread. By hand, begin stitching

¼" from the side edge of the petal and ¼" from the straight edge of the petal.

Make a tiny backstitch at the beginning to secure the knot so it cannot pop through the fabric when you pull the gathers. Make running stitches along the edge, using slightly less than a ¼" seam allowance so the gathering stitches will be hidden in the seam line when the petals are attached to the circle later on.

Pull stitches tightly as you go, creating puckers or gathers in the fabric.

Stitch to ¼" from the other edge of the petal, making enough gathers so that the petal measures ¾" along the straight edge. Make a backstitch and knot the thread to hold the gathers firmly in place. Repeat for all petals.

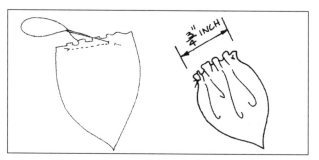

2. Holding the tree so the tip is down and the trunk is up, sew a gathered petal to the left side of each tree curve. Place the petal on top of the tree, right sides together. Pin the petal to the tree at both ends of the curve. Because these pieces are small and curved, you may find it easier to stitch the units together by hand. Begin stitching at the point of the petal and stitch toward the trunk of the tree using a small, tight, running stitch. Ease the fullness of the petal to fit the curve of the tree as you stitch. Clip ⅛" into the curve of the tree if necessary to fit the two pieces together.

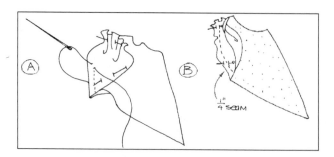

3. Pin triangles onto the right, straight sides of half of the trees so that the long sides of the

triangles face the left sides of the trees. Begin stitching at the trunk of each tree and stitch toward the tip. Press the seam toward the tree.

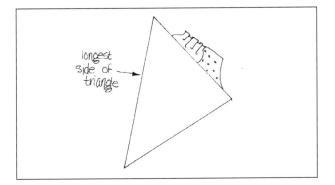

4. Sew squares to the right sides of the remaining trees. Begin sewing at the trunk of each tree and stitch toward the tip. (The tip of the tree will extend slightly beyond the end of the square.) Press the seam toward the tree.

5. Stitch a petal-tree-triangle unit to a petal-tree-square unit. Pin the units together near the center where the petal point meets the tree on one unit and the square meets the tree on the other unit. Have the petal-tree junction and the tree-square junction facing in opposite directions with the seams butted up against each other. Place a pin at this point to assure that the seams meet accurately and cannot shift during stitching. Place a second pin connecting the base of the petal and the trunk of the tree.

Handstitch the petal to the curve of the tree, starting at the trunk of the tree and stitching to the tip of the petal. Ease the petal to fit the curve, clipping ¹⁄₈" into the curve of the tree if necessary to ease the fullness. Handstitch to the tip of the petal. Continue stitching through the pinned joint and through the tree and the

triangle. (Straight stitching can be done more efficiently by machine.) Press the seam toward the tree. Continue this sequence until the block is completed.

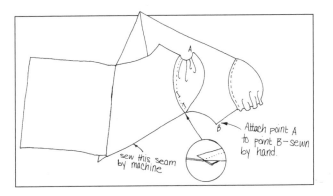

6. Fold the center circle in half and then into quarters to mark it into equal quadrants. Place a pin at each quarter point. Fit the circle into the round opening of the patch, having right sides together and fitting two petals into each quarter of the circle. Pin in place. Stitch around the circle through all thicknesses.

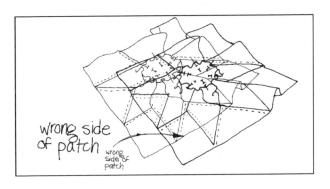

Joining the Patches

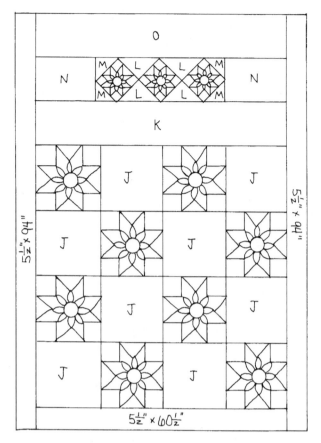

1. Sew a large Dahlia patch to a plain patch (J) making a horizontal row of 4 alternating patches. Repeat to make a second row.

2. Make another horizontal row of patches beginning with the opposite patch. Repeat to make a second row.

3. Sew the rows together so that the Dahlia patches and the plain patches alternate both vertically and horizontally.

4. Add section K to the joined patches.

5. Join section L to the Small Dahlia patches in the following sequence.

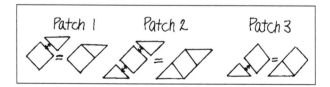

6. Join the Small Dahlia/section L units together.

7. Sew the M triangles to the ends of the Small Dahlia unit.

8. Sew the N blocks to the ends of the Small Dahlia unit.

9. Sew the Small Dahlia unit to the joined patch unit.

10. Sew section O to the top of the Small Dahlia unit.

11. Cut one border section from Fabric 4 measuring $5\frac{1}{2}$" wide x $60\frac{1}{2}$" long. (Note: Measure the bottom width of the joined patches and adjust the $60\frac{1}{2}$" measurement if necessary to fit your individual quilt.)

12. Attach the border to the lower edge of the joined patches.

13. Cut two border sections from Fabric 4 measuring $5\frac{1}{2}$" wide x 94" long. (Note: Measure the length of the joined patches and adjust the 94" measurement if necessary to fit your individual quilt.)

14. Attach the side borders to each side of the joined patches.

Making a Cone Border

The cone border is made up of three templates identified in the text as follows:

Cone G (Template on page 49)—
    cut 56 from Fabric 1
Cone H (Template on page 49)—
    cut 59 from Fabric 2
Cone I (Template on page 52-53)—
    cut 2 from Fabric 1

1. With right sides together, stitch Cone G to Cone H with the narrow points of the cones opposite each other. (The point of each cone will extend beyond the bottom of the cone to which it is attached.)

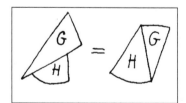

Continue this sequence to form one row of cones, having 15 of Cone H and 14 of Cone G.

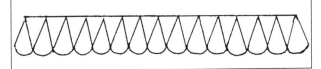

2. Attach the straight edge of the cone border to the bottom of the quilt, so that each bottom corner is met by the point of a Cone H.

3. Repeat the sequence for the side borders, having 22 of Cone H and 21 of Cone G on each row. Attach the borders to each side so that the point of Cone H is even with the corner of the quilt on each end. The Cone H that meets the top left corner of the quilt and the Cone H that meets the top right corner of the quilt will each need to be trimmed after the cone borders are attached. (That is necessary to make the top of the quilt straight.)

4. Use Cone I to fill in the border on the two bottom corners. Begin stitching at the curved end of the cone and stitch toward the point.

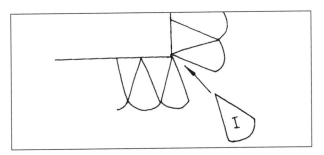

Marking Quilting Lines

Quilting designs are given for the plain patches that are attached to the pieced Dahlia patches (pages 55-56) and also for the inner border (pages 36-38).

Quilt the Dahlia patches and the cone border by outlining the pieced patches with quilting stitches along the seam lines. Outlined sections will look puffy when quilted.

Some of the quilting designs extend over several pages. Remove these pages and tape them together at the designated places to create a full quilting template.

Make all quilt markings as lightly as possible, since quilting goes over but does not cover marked lines.

Marking may be done by placing the design underneath the appropriate fabric and tracing lightly over the lines. You may also mark from the top by making your own template from cardboard or plastic and cutting slits for tracing the quilting lines.

You can make your own light table by placing a storm window or sheet of plexiglas over an open extension table with a lamp underneath.

1. Mark the quilting lines on each alternate block, centering the quilting motif within the patch.

2. Mark the quilting lines on the inner border, centering the quilting motif within the border width.

3. Mark diagonal lines on the pillow throw section, filling the open spaces with lines slanting toward a point at the center. Begin marking at the center V and work toward the outside, making lines approximately 1-1$\frac{1}{2}$" apart. A yardstick works well for spacing the diagonal lines evenly.

Quilting

You will need a backing fabric measuring at least 95" x 110," and batting of the same size.

Layer the backing, batting, and Dahlia top in a quilting frame, or baste the layers together securely so the layers will not shift if you will be using a small hoop.

The quilting stitch is a simple running stitch that pierces through all three layers of the quilt and holds them together. Quilting also creates a decorative pattern on the quilt and adds dimension to the pieced design.

Quilting is done with a single strand of quilting thread. Knot the thread and insert the needle through the top layer of the quilt, about one inch away from where the first quilting

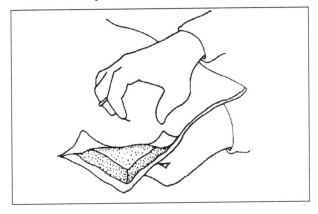

stitch will emerge on a marked line or along a seam line. Tug the knot gently through the top layer so it is hidden between the layers. Reinsert the needle into the fabric, going through all the layers. Quilting is a rocking motion, with the needle going up and down as it enters and exits the layers of the quilt.

When you have used an entire length of thread, make a small knot and again pop it through the top layer of fabric, burying it in the layers of the quilt.

The goal in quilting is to have small, even stitches that are equal in length on the top and bottom of the quilt. This is best achieved with hours of practice!

Binding

1. Before binding, baste the raw edges of the quilt together around the entire circumference of the quilt. Trim away excess batting and backing.

2. Cut 2¼"-wide bias binding to measure a total of about 475 inches in length. Fold the binding in half lengthwise wrong sides together and press.

3. Lay the binding strip along the scalloped edge of the quilt top, with the raw edges even and the fold of the binding facing the center of the quilt. Stitch the binding in place through all thicknesses using a ¼" seam allowance. Ease the binding around the curves, pivoting at the inside point of each scallop.

4. Fold the binding around to the back of the quilt, encasing all raw edges. Slip-stitch by hand, with the fold of the binding along the seam line.

Templates for Dahlia and Quilted Block Quilt

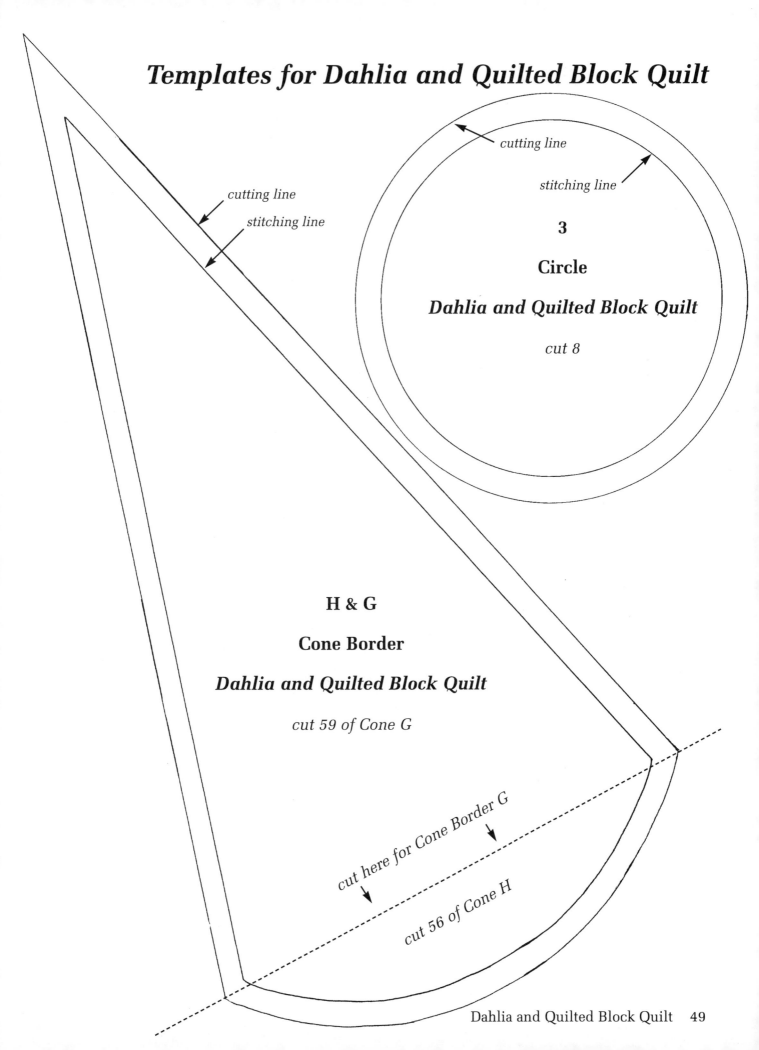

cutting line

stitching line

cutting line

stitching line

3

Circle

Dahlia and Quilted Block Quilt

cut 8

H & G

Cone Border

Dahlia and Quilted Block Quilt

cut 59 of Cone G

cut here for Cone Border G

cut 56 of Cone H

Templates for Dahlia and Quilted Block Quilt

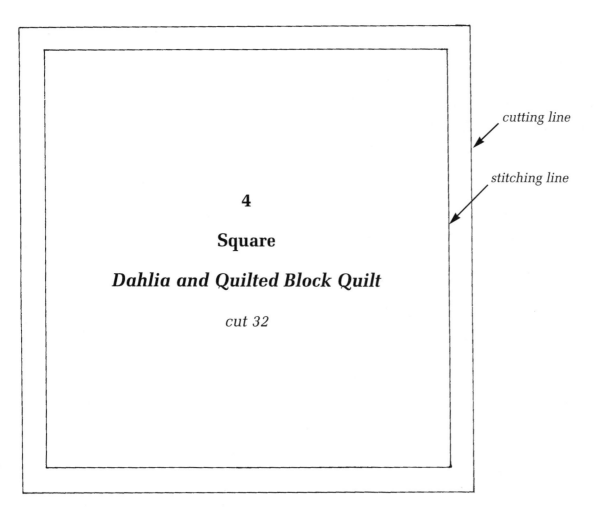

cutting line

stitching line

4

Square

Dahlia and Quilted Block Quilt

cut 32

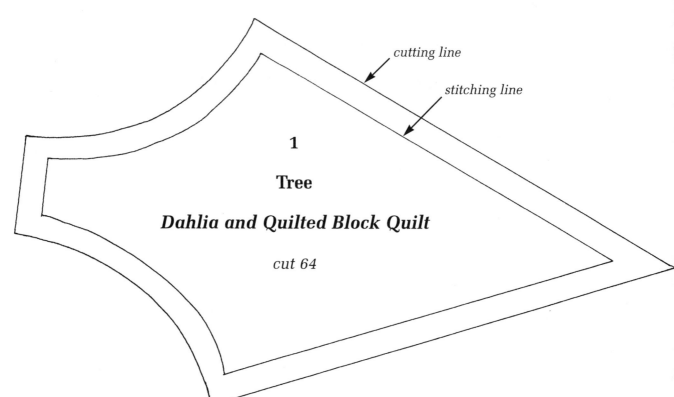

cutting line

stitching line

1

Tree

Dahlia and Quilted Block Quilt

cut 64

Templates for Dahlia and Quilted Block Quilt

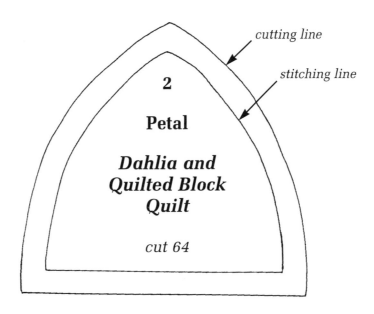

cutting line

stitching line

2

Petal

Dahlia and Quilted Block Quilt

cut 64

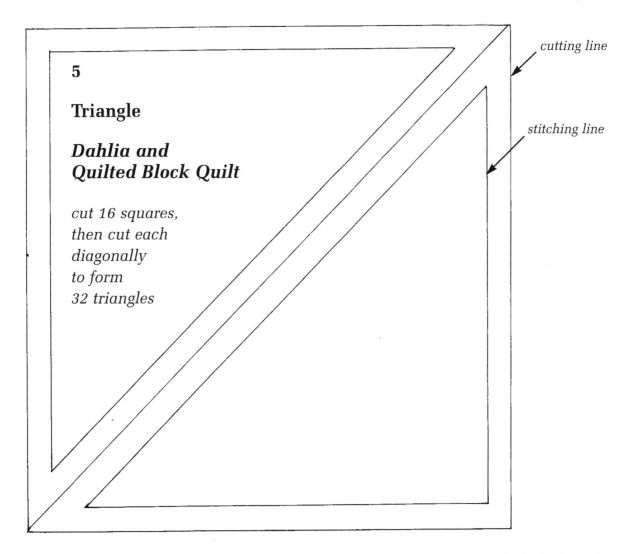

cutting line

stitching line

5

Triangle

Dahlia and Quilted Block Quilt

cut 16 squares, then cut each diagonally to form 32 triangles

Templates for Dahlia and Quilted Block Quilt

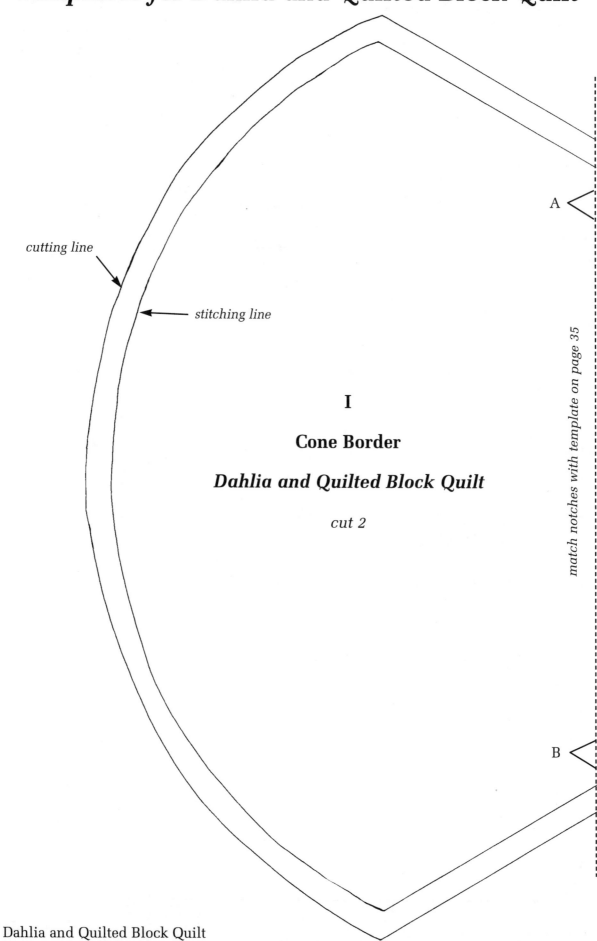

cutting line

stitching line

A

B

match notches with template on page 35

I

Cone Border

Dahlia and Quilted Block Quilt

cut 2

Templates for Dahlia and Quilted Block Quilt

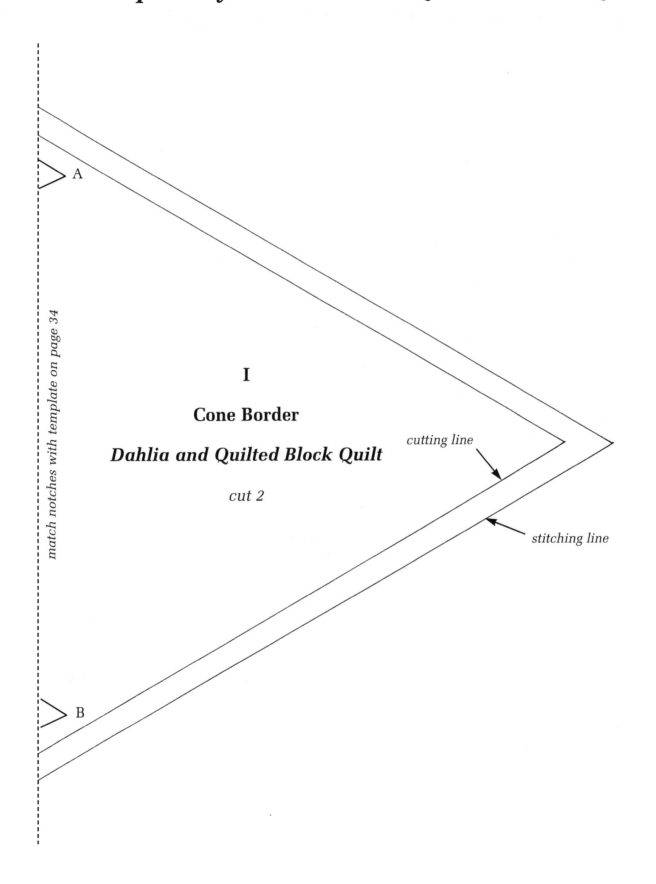

match notches with template on page 34

A

B

I

Cone Border

Dahlia and Quilted Block Quilt

cut 2

cutting line

stitching line

Pillow Throw Templates, Dahlia and Quilted Block Quilt

cutting line

stitching line

5

Triangle
Pillow Throw,
Dahlia and
Quilted Block
Quilt

cut 12

4

Square

Pillow Throw,
Dahlia and
Quilted Block Quilt

cut 12

cutting line

stitching line

1
Tree
Pillow Throw,
Dahlia and Quilted Block
Quilt
cut 24

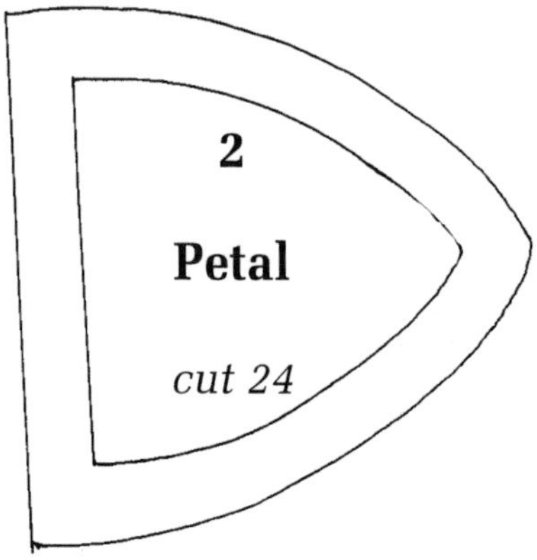

2

Petal

cut 24

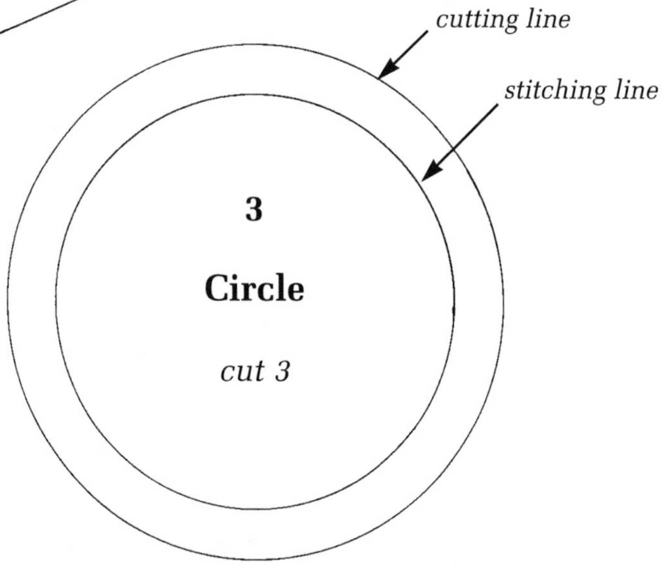

cutting line

stitching line

3

Circle

cut 3

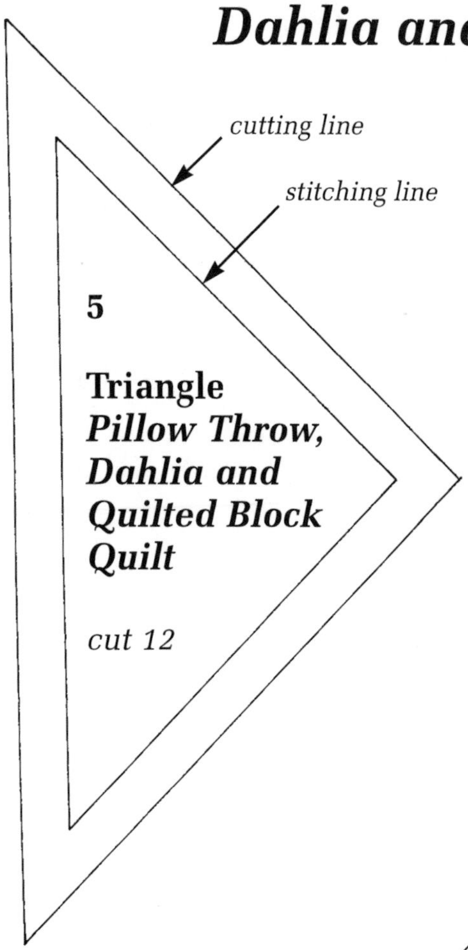

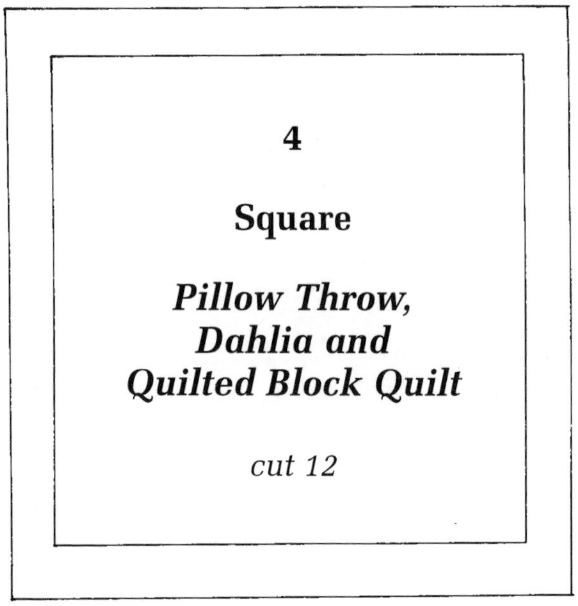

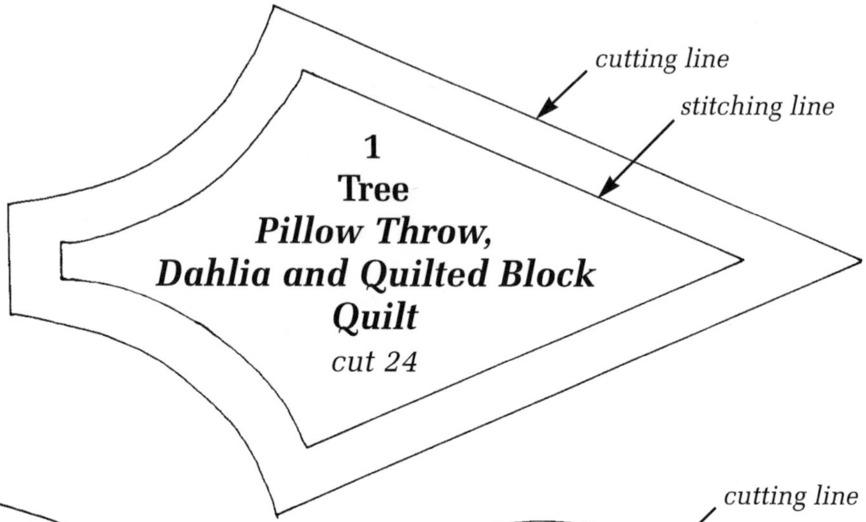

Quilting Template for Plain Patches, Dahlia and Quilted Block Quilt

(turn the template to create top part)

match notches with template on page 56

Quilting Template for Plain Patches, Dahlia and Quilted Block Quilt

(turn the template to create top part)

C

D

match notches with template on page 55

Dahlia Wallhanging

Finished size is approximately 18" x 23"

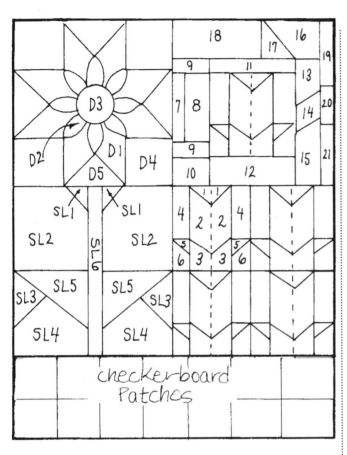

The Dahlia Wallhanging combines a small version of the Dahlia patch with pieced tulips, a watering can, and a checkerboard, to create a charming wall decoration.

Fabric Requirements

Fabric 1—Templates D1, D3, 1, 2—¼ yd.
Fabric 2—Templates D2, 1, 2—¹⁄₁₆ yd.
Fabric 3—Templates SL1, SL3, 3, 4, 5, 6, 7, 9, 11, 12, 14, 17, 20—⅛ yd.
Fabric 4—Template 2, Checkerboard—⅛ yd.
Fabric 5—Templates D5, SL5, SL6, 3, 5—⅛ yd.
Fabric 6—Template 1, Checkerboard—⅛ yd.
Fabric 7—Templates D4, D5, SL2, SL4—¼ yd.
Fabric 8—Templates 4, 6, 8, 10, 13, 15, 16, 18, 19, 21—⅛ yd.
Backing—21" x 26"
Batting—21" x 26"

Making the Pieced Tulip Block

Pieced tulips appear along the right side of the wallhanging. The pieced tulip templates are numbered 1 through 6 and should be cut as follows (see photo on page 40):

Template 1 (page 63 for cutting instructions)
Template 2 (page 63 for cutting instructions)
Template 3 (page 63 for cutting instructions)
Template 4 (page 63 for cutting instructions)
Template 5 (page 63 for cutting instructions)
Template 6 (page 63 for cutting instructions)

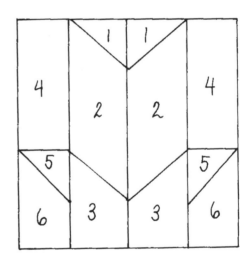

1. Sew Template 1 to Template 2.

2. Sew the 1,2 unit to Template 3.

3. Sew Template 5 to Template 6.

4. Sew the 5,6 unit to Template 4.

5. Sew the 1,2,3 unit to the 4,5,6 unit.

6. Repeat steps 1 through 5, using the pieces cut in the opposite direction.

7. Sew the two halves of the tulip patch together.

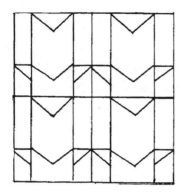

Connecting the Tulip Blocks

After the five pieced tulips are constructed, they should be put together as follows:

1. Join one tulip block with another horizontally.

2. Repeat step 1.

3. Sew the two strips of tulip blocks together to make a patch with 4 tulip patches.

(The remaining pieced tulip will be part of the watering can block.)

Making the Watering Can Block

The Watering Can Block consists of the pieced tulip block plus 15 templates which are numbered 7-21 on pages 63-65) **Cut 2 of Template 9 and one of each of the others.**

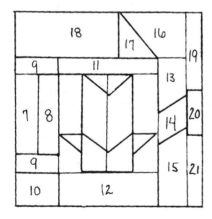

1. Sew Template 7 and Template 8 together.

2. Sew one Template 9 to the top and the other Template 9 to the bottom of the 7,8 unit.

3. Sew Template 10 to the 7,8,9 unit.

4. Sew Template 11 to the top of the pieced tulip block.

5. Sew Template 12 to the bottom of the pieced tulip block.

6. Sew the 7,8,9,10 unit to the left side of the pieced tulip block.

7. Sew Template 13 to the top of Template 14.

8. Sew Template 15 to the bottom of the 13,14 unit.

9. Sew the 13,14,15 unit to the right side of the pieced tulip block.

10. Sew Template 16 to Template 17.

11. Sew the 16,17 unit to Template 18.

12. Sew the 16,17,18 unit to the top of the pieced tulip block.

13. Sew Template 19 to the top of Template 20.

14. Sew Template 21 to the bottom of the 19,20 unit.

15. Sew the 19,20,21 unit to the right side of the pieced tulip block.

Making the Dahlia Patch

The vertical patch on the left side of the wallhanging uses a small version of the Traditional Dahlia patch. The Dahlia is made up of five templates which will be identified in the instructions as follows:

1. Trees—(page 66) cut 8 of Fabric 1
2. Petals—(page 66) cut 8 of Fabric 2
3. Circle—(page 66) cut 1 of Fabric 1
4. Squares—(page 66) cut 4 of Fabric 7
5. Triangles—(page 66) cut 3 of Fabric 7; cut 1 of Fabric 5

1. Make gathers along the straight edge of the petals. To do so, use a double strand of thread and a medium sized needle. Make a knot at the end of the thread. By hand, begin stitching $\frac{1}{4}$" from the side edge of the petal and $\frac{1}{4}$" from the straight edge of the petal.

Make a tiny backstitch at the beginning to secure the knot so it cannot pop through the fabric when you pull the gathers. Make running stitches along the edge, using slightly less than a $\frac{1}{4}$" seam allowance so the gathering stitches will be hidden in the seam line when the petals are attached to the circle later on.

Pull stitches tightly as you go, creating puckers or gathers in the fabric.

Stitch to ¼" from the other edge of the petal, making enough gathers so that the petal measures ¾" along the straight edge. Make a backstitch and knot the thread to hold the gathers firmly in place. Repeat for all petals.

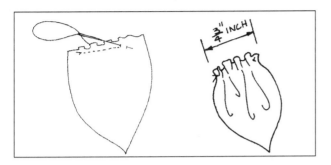

2. Holding the tree so the tip is down and the trunk is up, sew a gathered petal to the left side of each tree curve. Place the petal on top of the tree, right sides together. Pin the petal to the tree at both ends of the curve. Because these pieces are small and curved, you may find it easier to stitch the units together by hand. Begin stitching at the point of the petal and stitch toward the trunk of the tree using a small, tight, running stitch. Ease the fullness of the petal to fit the curve of the tree as you stitch. Clip ⅛" into the curve of the tree if necessary to fit the two pieces together.

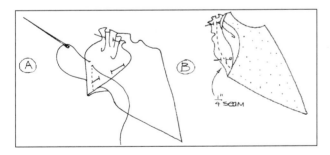

3. Pin triangles onto the right, straight sides of half of the trees so that the long sides of

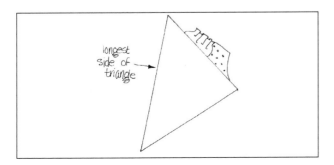

the triangles face the left sides of the trees. Begin stitching at the trunk of each tree and stitch toward the tip. Press the seam toward the tree.

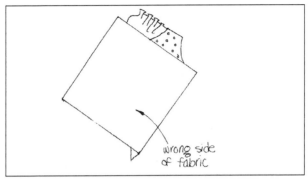

4. Sew squares to the right sides of the remaining trees. Begin sewing at the trunk of each tree and stitch toward the tip. (The tip of the tree will extend slightly beyond the end of the square.) Press the seam toward the tree.

5. Stitch a petal-tree-triangle unit to a petal-tree-square unit. Pin the units together near the center where the petal point meets the tree on one unit and the square meets the tree on the other unit. Have the petal-tree junction and the tree-square junction facing in opposite directions with the seams butted up against each other. Place a pin at this point to assure that the seams meet accurately and cannot shift during stitching. Place a second pin connecting the base of the petal and the trunk of the tree.

Handstitch the petal to the curve of the tree, starting at the base of the tree and stitching to the tip of the petal. Ease the petal to fir the curve, clipping ⅛" into the curve of the tree if necessary to ease the fullness. Handstitch to the tip of the petal. Continue stitching through the pinned joint and through the tree and the

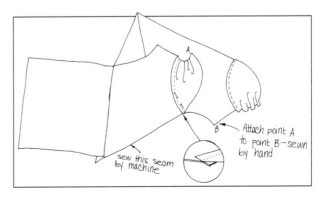

triangle. (Straight stitching can be done more efficiently by machine.) Press the seam toward the tree. Continue the sequence of joining units until the block is completed.

6. Fold the center circle in half and then into quarters to mark it into equal quadrants. Place a pin at each quarter point. Fit the circle into the round opening of the patch, having right sides together and fitting two petals into each quarter of the circle. Pin in place. Stitch around the circle through all thicknesses.

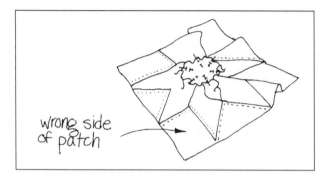

Making the Stem and Leaf Block

The Stem and Leaf Block consists of 6 templates that should be cut as follows:

Template SL1 (see page 67 for cutting
   instructions)
Template SL2 (see page 67 for cutting
   instructions)
Template SL3 (see page 67 for cutting
   instructions)
Template SL4 (see page 67 for cutting
   instructions)
Template SL5 (see page 67 for cutting
   instructions)
Template SL6 (see page 67 for cutting
   instructions)

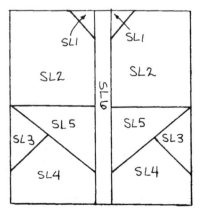

1. Sew Template SL1 to Template SL2. Repeat with opposite templates.

2. Sew Template SL3 to Template SL4. Repeat with opposite templates.

3. Sew the SL3,4 unit to Template SL5. Repeat with opposite templates.

4. Sew the SL1,2 unit to the SL3,4,5 unit. Repeat with opposite templates.

5. Sew Template SL6 between the SL1,2,3,4,5 units.

Making the Checkerboard

The Checkerboard consists of contrasting squares attached to each other in alternate rows. The Checkerboard requires one square template.

Checkerboard Template (page 65)—cut 7 of Fabric 4 and 7 of Fabric 6.

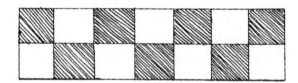

1. Sew 7 of the blocks together using alternating fabrics.

2. Repeat step 1, beginning with contrasting fabric.

3. Join the two rows of blocks to create the Checkerboard.

Connecting the Blocks

1. Sew the Dahlia Block to the top of the Stem/Leaf block, so that the green triangle of the Dahlia lies against the stem on the Stem/Leaf Block.

2. Sew the Watering Can Block to the top of the Pieced Tulip Block.

3. Sew the Stem and Leaf Block to the Watering Can and Tulip Blocks.

4. Sew the Checkerboard to the bottom of the pieced blocks.

Quilting

The quilting on the wallhanging should outline the patchwork design to emphasis the pieced shapes. Quilt along the seams to outline the Dahlia, the Dahlia Stem and Leaves, the Watering Can, and each pieced Tulip. The Checkerboard may be done by outlining each square, or by crossing each square diagonally to create an X in each square of the Checkerboard.

Layer the backing, batting, and wallhanging top in a quilting frame, or baste the layers together securely so the layers will not shift if you will be using a small hoop.

The quilting stitch is a simple running stitch that pierces through all three layers of the quilt and holds them together. Quilting also creates a decorative pattern on the quilt and adds dimension to the pieced design.

Quilting is done with a single strand of quilting thread. Knot the thread and insert the needle through the top layer of the quilt, about one inch away from where the first quilting stitch will emerge on a marked line or along a seam line. Tug the knot gently through the top layer so it is hidden between the layers. Reinsert the needle into the fabric, going through all the layers. Quilting is a rocking motion, with the needle going up and down as it enters and exits the layers of the quilt.

When you have used an entire length of thread, make a small knot and again pop it through the top layer of fabric, burying it in the layers of the quilt.

The goal in quilting is to have small, even stitches that are equal in length on the top and bottom of the quilt. This is best achieved with hours of practice!

Binding

Because the wallhanging has straight edges, you do not need to cut the binding strips on the bias.

Cut 2 strips of Fabric 2 measuring 2" wide x 19" long.

Cut 2 strips of Fabric 2 measuring 2" wide x 27" long.

1. Fold the binding strips in half lengthwise with the wrong sides together. Press.

2. Place the raw edges of one of the shorter binding strips even with the raw edge of the wallhanging top. (The folded edge of the binding should face toward the center of the wallhanging.)

Sew the binding to the top.

Trim the excess batting and backing even with the edge of the binding and the wallhanging top.

Fold the binding up so the folded edges of the binding strip extend beyond the raw edges of the wallhanging top.

Sew the second shorter strip to the bottom of the wallhanging, following the above procedure.

3. Sew the remaining binding strips along the two sides of the wallhanging, again with the raw edges of the binding even with the raw edge of the quilt top. Stitch from one end to the other, including the extended bindings on the top and bottom of the wallhanging. Trim the excess back and batting even with the wallhanging top.

4. Fold the bindings around to the back side of the wallhanging with the fold of the binding even with the stitching line and encasing all the raw edges. Using a blindstitch, handstitch the binding in place, doing the top and bottom edges first. Trim excess binding at corners to eliminate bulk, and fold corners to encase all raw edges. Blindstitch side bindings in place.

5. Handstitch small loops or a narrow casing on the back of the wallhanging so it can be hung.

Tulip Block Templates for Dahlia Wallhanging

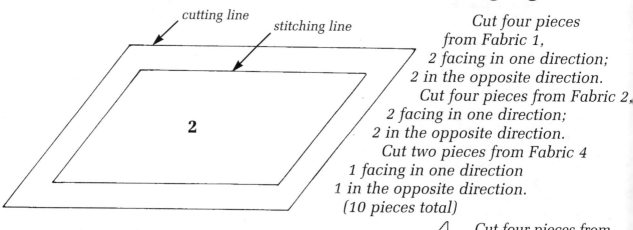

cutting line

stitching line

Cut four pieces from Fabric 1, 2 facing in one direction; 2 in the opposite direction. Cut four pieces from Fabric 2, 2 facing in one direction; 2 in the opposite direction. Cut two pieces from Fabric 4 1 facing in one direction 1 in the opposite direction. (10 pieces total)

Cut four pieces from Fabric 3, 2 facing in one direction; 2 in the opposite direction.
Cut six pieces from Fabric 5, 3 facing in one direction; 3 in the opposite direction.
(10 pieces total)

Cut four pieces from Fabric 1, 2 facing in one direction; 2 in the opposite direction.
Cut four pieces from Fabric 2, 2 facing in one direction; 2 in the opposite direction.
Cut two pieces from Fabric 6, 1 facing in one direction; 1 in the opposite direction.
(10 pieces total)

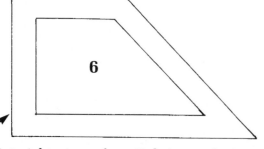

Cut eight pieces from Fabric 8, 4 facing in one direction; 4 in the opposite direction.
Cut two pieces from Fabric 3, 1 facing in one direction; 1 in the opposite direction.
(10 pieces total)

Cut eight pieces from Fabric 8 and two pieces from Fabric 3. (10 pieces total)

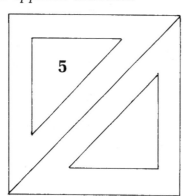

Cut two squares from Fabric 3 and three squares from Fabric 5. Then cut each diagonally. (10 pieces total)

Watering Can Templates for Dahlia Wallhanging

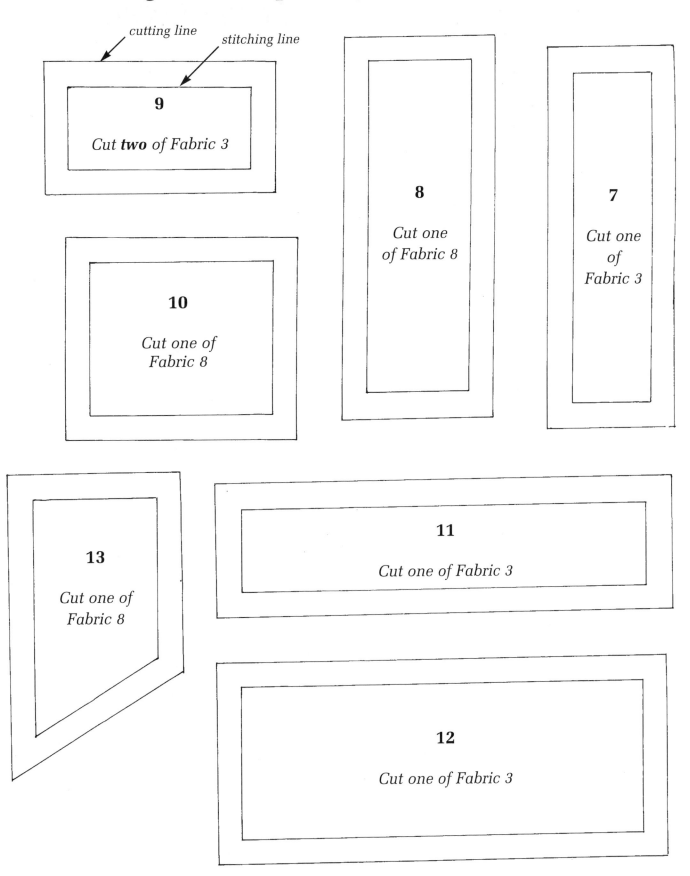

cutting line

stitching line

9

Cut **two** of Fabric 3

8

Cut one
of Fabric 8

7

Cut one
of
Fabric 3

10

Cut one of
Fabric 8

13

Cut one of
Fabric 8

11

Cut one of Fabric 3

12

Cut one of Fabric 3

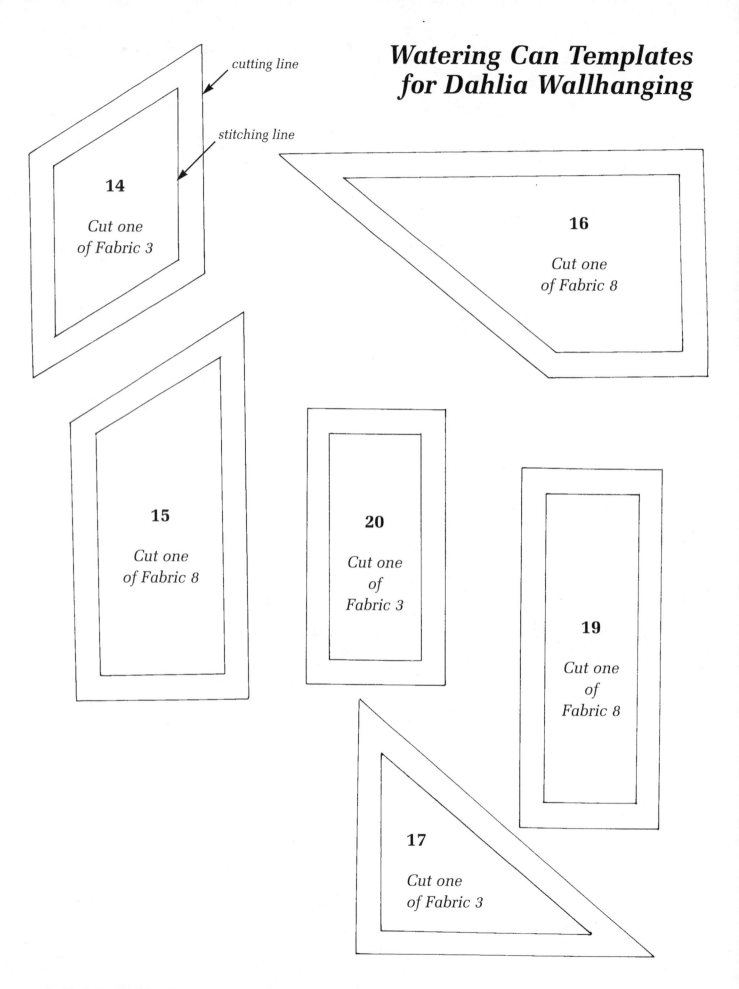

cutting line

stitching line

Watering Can Templates for Dahlia Wallhanging

14

Cut one of Fabric 3

16

Cut one of Fabric 8

15

Cut one of Fabric 8

20

Cut one of Fabric 3

19

Cut one of Fabric 8

17

Cut one of Fabric 3

Watering Can Templates for Dahlia Wallhanging

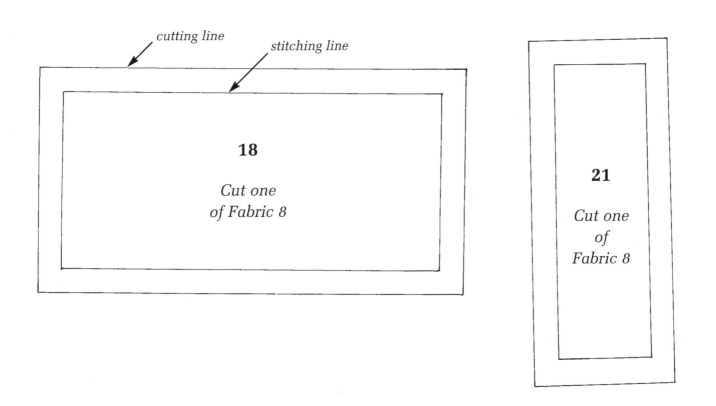

cutting line

stitching line

18

*Cut one
of Fabric 8*

21

*Cut one
of
Fabric 8*

Checkerboard Template for Dahlia Wallhanging

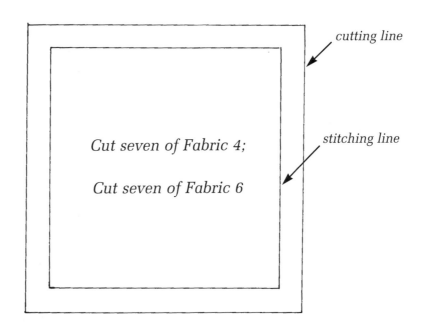

cutting line

stitching line

Cut seven of Fabric 4;

Cut seven of Fabric 6

Dahlia Templates for Dahlia Wallhanging

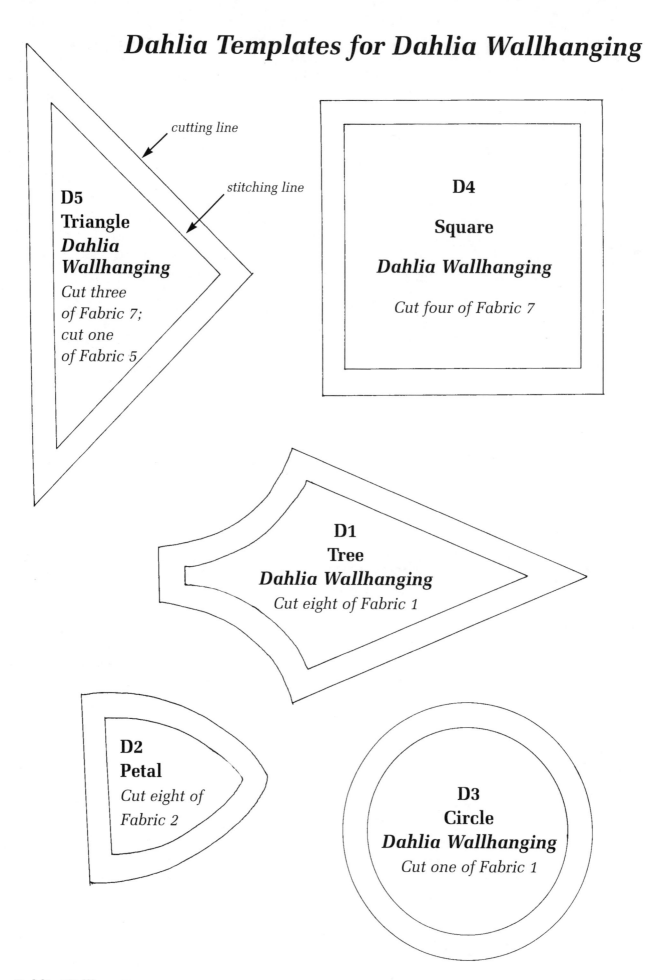

cutting line

stitching line

D5
Triangle
Dahlia
Wallhanging

Cut three
of Fabric 7;
cut one
of Fabric 5

D4

Square

Dahlia Wallhanging

Cut four of Fabric 7

D1
Tree
Dahlia Wallhanging

Cut eight of Fabric 1

D2
Petal

Cut eight of
Fabric 2

D3
Circle
Dahlia Wallhanging

Cut one of Fabric 1

Stem and Leaf Block Templates
for Dahlia Wallhanging

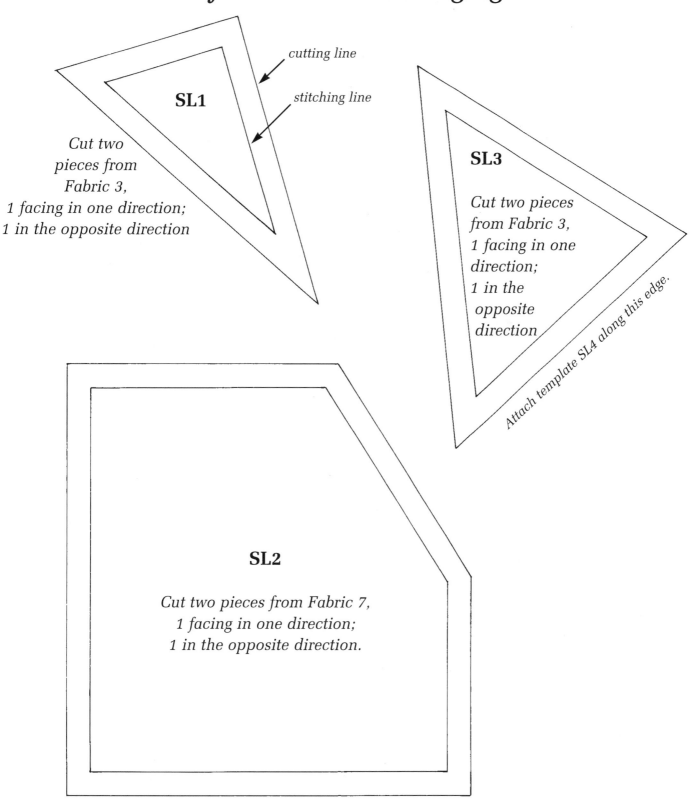

cutting line

stitching line

SL1

Cut two pieces from Fabric 3, 1 facing in one direction; 1 in the opposite direction

SL3

Cut two pieces from Fabric 3, 1 facing in one direction; 1 in the opposite direction

Attach template SL4 along this edge.

SL2

Cut two pieces from Fabric 7, 1 facing in one direction; 1 in the opposite direction.

Stem and Leaf Block Templates for Wallhanging

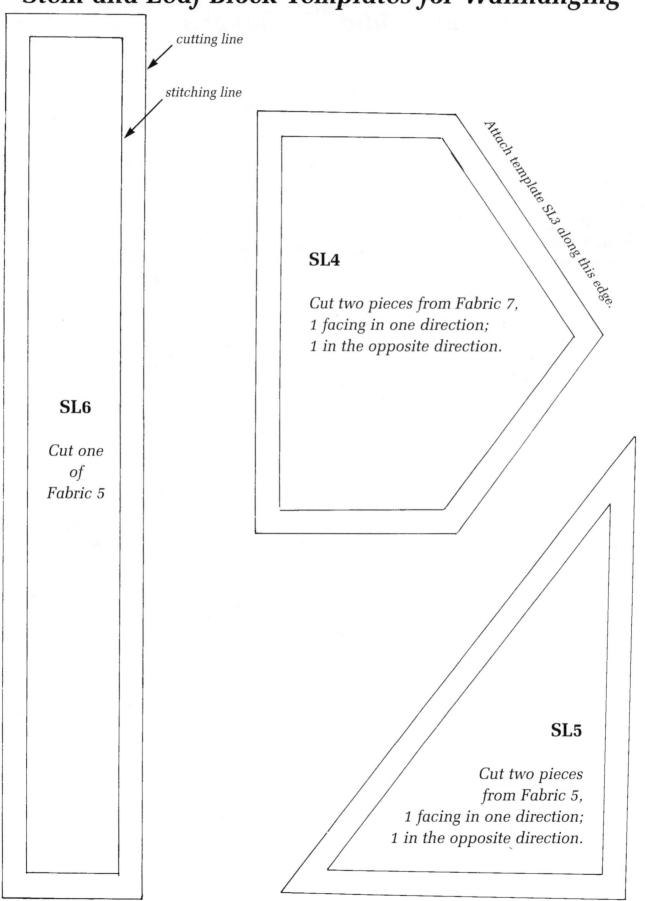

cutting line

stitching line

SL4

*Cut two pieces from Fabric 7,
1 facing in one direction;
1 in the opposite direction.*

Attach template SL3 along this edge.

SL6

*Cut one
of
Fabric 5*

SL5

*Cut two pieces
from Fabric 5,
1 facing in one direction;
1 in the opposite direction.*

Hot Pad

Finished size is approximately 9" square

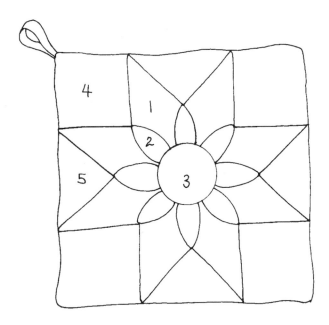

Fabric Requirements

Fabric 1—Templates 2, 4, 5, back—¹/₄ yd.
Fabric 2—Templates 1, 3—¹/₈ yd.
Batting—2-11" squares
4" grosgrain ribbon or double-fold bias tape

Making the Dahlia Patch

The Dahlia patch is made up of five shapes which will be identified in the text as follows:

1. Trees (Template 1, page 72)—
   cut 8 from Fabric 2
2. Petals (Template 2, page 72)—
   cut 8 from Fabric 1
3. Circle (Template 3, page 72)—
   cut 1 from Fabric 2
4. Squares (Template 4, page 72)—
   cut 4 from Fabric 1
5. Triangles (Template 5, page 72)—
   cut 4 from Fabric 1

1. Make gathers along the straight edge of the petals. To do so, use a double strand of thread and a medium sized needle. Make a knot at the end of the thread. By hand, begin stitching ¹/₄" from the side edge of the petal and ¹/₄" from the straight edge of the petal.

Make a tiny backstitch at the beginning to secure the knot so it cannot pop through the fabric when you pull the gathers. Make running stitches along the edge, using slightly less than a ¹/₄" seam allowance so the gathering stitches will be hidden in the seam line when the petals are attached to the circle later on.

Pull stitches tightly as you go, creating

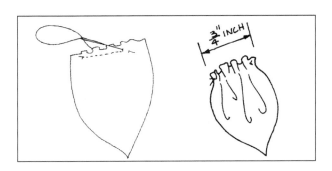

puckers or gathers in the fabric.

Stitch to ¼" from the other edge of the petal, making enough gathers so that the petal measures ¾" along the straight edge. Make a backstitch and knot the thread to hold the gathers firmly in place. Repeat for all petals.

2. Holding the tree so the tip is down and the trunk is up, sew a gathered petal to the left side of each tree curve. Place the petal on top of the tree, right sides together. Pin the petal to the tree at both ends of the curve. Because these pieces are small and curved, you may find it easier to stitch the units together by hand. Begin stitching at the point of the petal and stitch toward the trunk of the tree using a small, tight, running stitch. Ease the fullness of the petal to fit the curve of the tree as you stitch. Clip ⅛" into the curve of the tree if necessary to fit the two pieces together.

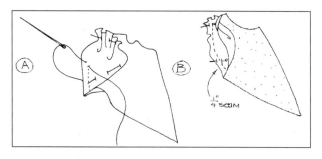

3. Pin triangles onto the right, straight sides of half of the trees so that the long sides of the triangles face the left sides of the trees. Begin stitching at the trunk of each tree and stitch toward the tip. Press the seam toward the tree.

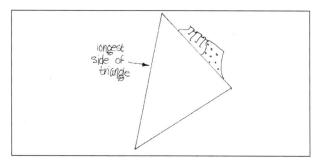

4. Sew squares to the right sides of the remaining trees. Begin sewing at the trunk of each tree and stitch toward the tip. (The tip of the tree will extend slightly beyond the end of the square.) Press the seam toward the tree.

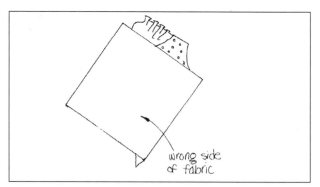

5. Stitch a petal-tree-triangle unit to a petal-tree-square unit. Pin the units together near the center where the petal point meets the tree on one unit and the square meets the tree on the other unit. Have the petal-tree junction and the tree-square junction facing in opposite directions with the seams butted up against each other. Place a pin at this point to assure that the seams meet accurately and cannot shift during stitching. Place a second pin connecting the base of the petal and the trunk of the tree.

Handstitch the petal to the curve of the tree, starting at the base of the tree and stitching to the tip of the petal. Ease the petal to fir the curve, clipping ⅛" into the curve of the tree if necessary to ease the fullness. Handstitch to the tip of the petal. Continue stitching through the pinned joint and through the tree and the triangle. (Straight stitching can be done more efficiently by machine.) Press the seam toward the tree. Continue the sequence of joining units until the block is completed.

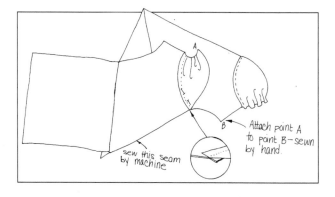

6. Fold the center circle in half and then into quarters to mark it into equal quadrants.

Place a pin at each quarter point. Fit the circle into the round opening of the patch, having right sides together and fitting two petals into each quarter of the circle. Pin in place. Stitch around the circle through all thicknesses.

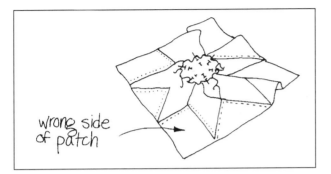

wrong side of patch

Adding the Batting

Cut a double layer of batting the same size as the small Dahlia patch. Place the two layers of batting against the wrong side of the small Dahlia patch.

Adding the Back

1. Cut a 4" length of double-fold bias tape or grosgrain ribbon that coordinates in color with the Dahlia patch.

2. Make a loop with the ribbon, bringing the cut ends together. Place the cut ends against the raw edge of the pieced patch. Pin in place.

3. Cut a piece of backing from Fabric 1 the same size as the small Dahlia patch.

4. Place the backing on top of the Dahlia, right sides together. Pin and stitch through all layers, leaving a $3^{1}/_{2}$" opening along one edge for turning. Trim away excess batting. Turn hot pad right side out. Slipstitch opening.

Dahlia Hot Pad Templates

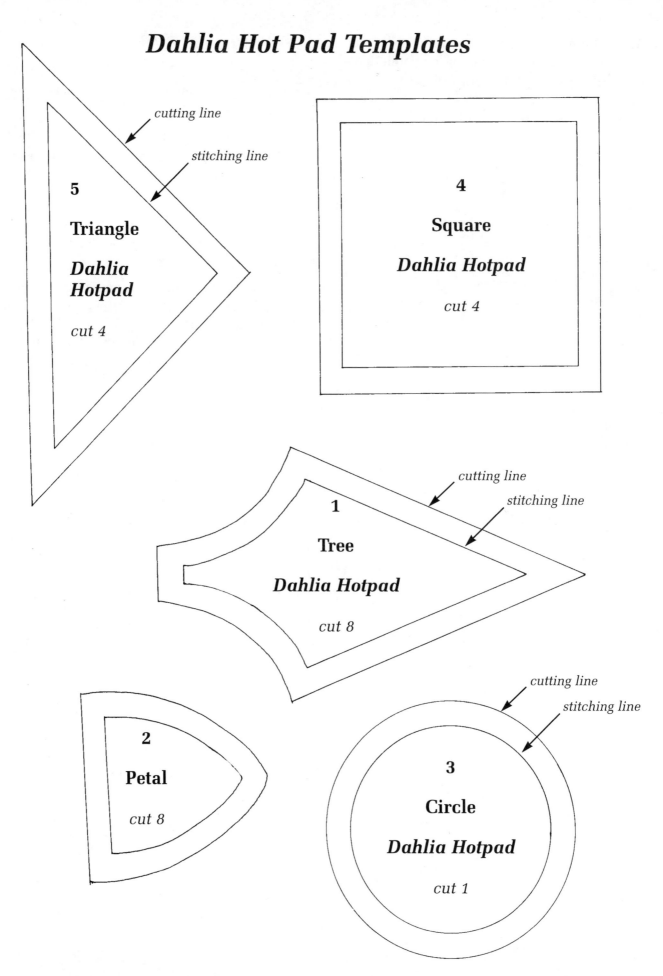

cutting line

stitching line

5

Triangle

Dahlia Hotpad

cut 4

4

Square

Dahlia Hotpad

cut 4

cutting line

stitching line

1

Tree

Dahlia Hotpad

cut 8

2

Petal

cut 8

cutting line

stitching line

3

Circle

Dahlia Hotpad

cut 1

Dahlia Hot Pad
(pattern begins on page 69)

Dahlia Quillow
*(pattern begins
on page 75)*

Dahlia Pillow and Dahlia Chair Pad
(pattern begins on page 89)

Dahlia Apron
(pattern begins on page 94)
and
Dahlia Table Runner
(pattern begins on page 81)

Dahlia Placemat
(pattern begins on page 85)

Dahlia Quillow

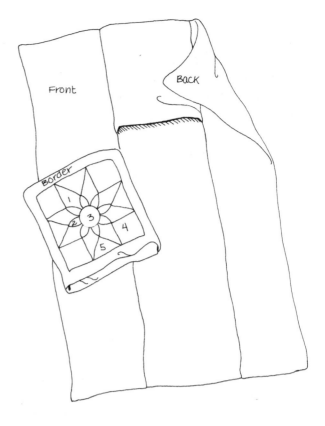

A "Quillow" combines a quilt and a pillow. When opened, it functions as a small quilt—a perfect size for snuggling on the sofa, relaxing while traveling in the car, or lounging in a dorm room. Folded together, the quillow disguises itself as a comfy and beautiful pillow that can be both decorative and functional.

Fabric Requirements

Fabric 1—Templates 1, 3, border, Quillow back—2³⁄₄ yds.
Fabric 2—Template 2—¹⁄₈ yd.
Fabric 3—Templates 4, 5, Quillow front—2 yds.
Batting—45" x 65" plus a 22" square

Cutting Instructions for Front and Back

1. Cut the front 45" wide x 65" long from Fabric 3 and lay aside.

2. Cut the back 45" wide x 65" long from Fabric 1 and lay aside.

Making the Dahlia Patch

The Traditional Dahlia patch is made up of five shapes which will be identified in the text as follows:

1. Tree—(Template 1, page 79) cut 8 of Fabric 1
2. Petal—(Template 2, page 80) cut 8 of Fabric 2
3. Circle—(Template 3, page 80) cut 1 of Fabric 1
4. Square—(Template 4, page 79) cut 4 of Fabric 3
5. Triangle—(Template 5, page 80) cut 2 squares of Fabric 3, then cut each diagonally to form 4 triangles

1. Make gathers along the straight edge of the petals. To do so, use a double strand of thread and a medium sized needle. Make a knot at the end of the thread. By hand, begin stitching ¹⁄₄" from the side edge of the petal and ¹⁄₄" from the straight edge of the petal.

Make a tiny backstitch at the beginning to secure the knot so it cannot pop through the fabric when you pull the gathers. Make running stitches along the edge, using slightly less than a ¹⁄₄" seam allowance so the gathering stitches will be hidden in the seam line when the petals are attached to the circle later on.

Pull stitches tightly as you go, creating puckers or gathers in the fabric.

Stitch to ¼" from the other edge of the petal, making enough gathers so that the petal measures 1" along the straight edge. Make a backstitch and knot the thread to hold the gathers firmly in place. Repeat for all petals.

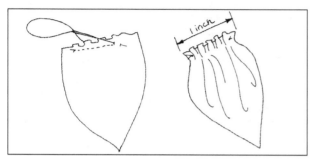

2. Holding the tree so the tip is down and the trunk is up, sew a gathered petal to the left side of each tree curve. Place the petal on top of the tree, right sides together. Pin the petal to the tree at both ends (A). Begin stitching at the point of the petal and stitch toward the tree trunk. Ease the fullness of the petal to fit the curve of the tree as you stitch (B).

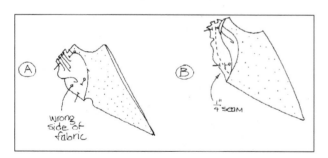

3. Pin triangles onto the right, straight sides of 4 of the trees so that the long sides of the triangles face the left sides of the trees. Begin stitching at the trunk of each tree and stitch toward the tip. Press the seam toward the tree.

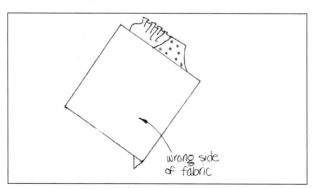

4. Sew squares to the right sides of the remaining 4 trees. Begin sewing at the trunk of each tree and stitch toward the tip. (The tip of the tree will extend slightly beyond the end of the square.) Press the seam toward the tree.

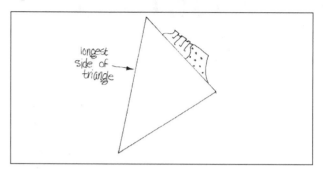

5. Stitch a petal-tree-triangle unit to a petal-tree-square unit. Pin the units together near the center where the petal point meets the tree on one unit and the square meets the tree on the other unit. Have the petal-tree junction and the tree-square junction facing in opposite directions with the seams butted up against each other. Place a pin at this point to assure that the seams meet accurately and cannot shift during stitching. Place a second pin connecting the base of the petal and the trunk of the tree.

With the petal on top, begin stitching at the trunk of the tree, easing the petal to fit the curve. Continue stitching over the pinned joint and through the end of the tree and triangle. Press the seam toward the tree. Continue this sequence until a square patch is completed.

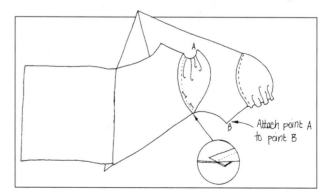

6. Fold the center circle in half and then into quarters to mark it into equal quadrants. Place a pin at each quarter point. Fit the circle into the round opening of the patch having right sides together and fitting two petals into each quarter of the circle. Pin in place. Stitch around the circle through all thicknesses.

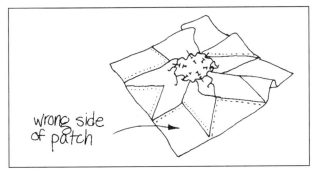

wrong side of patch

7. Enlarge the Dahlia patch by adding a border on all sides. To do so, cut 2 strips (A) of Fabric 1, 3" wide x the exact width of the finished patch. Attach these strips to the top and bottom of the patch. Cut 2 more strips (B) measuring 3 inches wide x the length of the patch, including the top and bottom borders. Attach these strips to the remaining sides. Press seams toward outer edges.

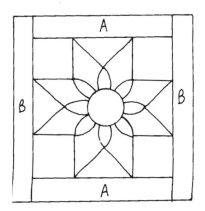

Making the Pillow

1. Cut a square of Fabric 1 for the back of the "pillow," measuring the same size as the completed Dahlia patch. This fabric will lay on top of the "quilt" back.

2. Cut a square of batting the same size as the "pillow" front and back.

Assembling the Quillow

1. Place the square of batting on a smooth flat surface, being sure that it is flat and wrinkle-free. Place the Dahlia patch on top of the batting with the wrong side against the batting. Place the back of the pillow over the Dahlia patch with the right side facing the Dahlia. Pin the three layers together to prevent any shifting while stitching.

2. Using a ¹/₂" seam allowance, stitch the three layers of the pillow together on three sides. Let the fourth side open. Trim excess batting from edges and corners. Turn the pillow right side out. Hand or machine quilt around the outline of the star, very close to the seam line.

3. Fold the quilt back in half lengthwise to find the center point of the fabric. Mark this point with a pin along the bottom edge. Do the same to establish the center point of the pillow along the open edge.

4. Lay the quilt back, right side up, on a smooth flat surface.
    Match the pins at the center points of the quilt back and the pillow. The raw edges of the pillow should be even with the bottom raw edge of the quilt back. The Dahlia side of

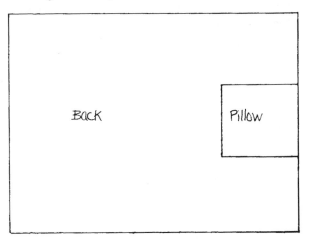

the pillow should face the right side of the quilt back. Pin the pillow securely to the quilt back.

5. Stitch the pillow to the quilt back along the right and left sides of the pillow. Stitch as close to the edge as possible, backstitching at the top of the pillow to secure the stitching.

6. Mark two straight lines on the quilt back, starting at the lower edge ¼" inside the stitching line where the pillow is attached to the quilt back and extending all the way to the top edge of the quilt back. (These lines will later serve as a machine quilting line.)

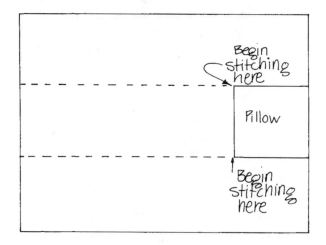

7. Cut a piece of batting measuring the exact width and length of the quilt back and front. Place the batting on a smooth flat surface, being sure it is wrinkle-free. Smooth the quilt top over the batting with the wrong side of the quilt top against the batting and the right side facing up.

Layer the quilt back over the top with the right side of the quilt back (pillow attached) facing the right side of the quilt top.

Pin the layers together, placing pins at close intervals along all four edges so there is no possibility of the layers shifting while stitching.

8. Using a ½" seam allowance, begin stitching along the top of the quillow, 18" from the outer edge. Stitch around three sides of the quilt through all layers and continue stitching 18" from the opposite side of the top.

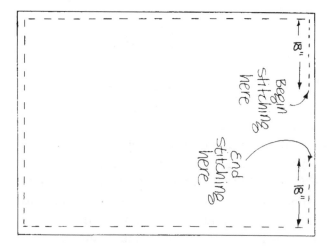

Backstitch at both the beginning and the end of the stitching. Leave the center section of the quillow top open for turning.

9. Turn quillow right side out. Fold seam allowances along opening at the top edge to the inside. Close the opening by machine stitching as close to the edge as possible.

10. Beginning at the lower edge of the quilt and working toward the top, machine quilt through all layers on the previously marked straight lines. This will stabilize the batting and help to prevent it from migrating.

11. Lay the quillow flat with the front facing you and the pillow on the back. Fold the sides toward the center along the stitched lines. Fold the quilt down from the top in thirds. Turn the pillow "inside out," bringing the Dahlia side of the pillow to the outside and having the quilt tucked inside the pillow.

Templates for Dahlia Quillow

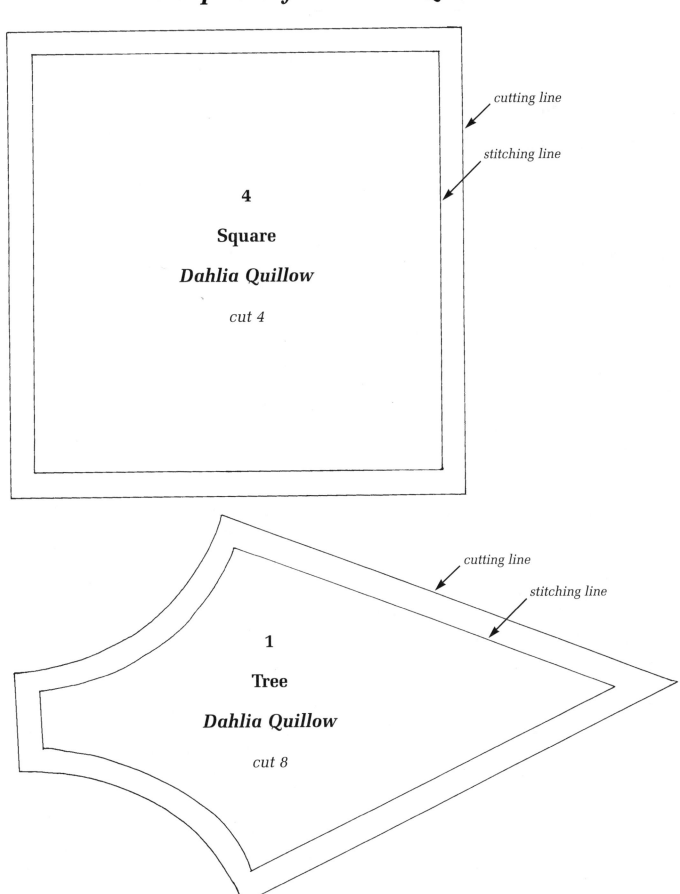

cutting line

stitching line

4

Square

Dahlia Quillow

cut 4

cutting line

stitching line

1

Tree

Dahlia Quillow

cut 8

Templates for Dahlia Quillow

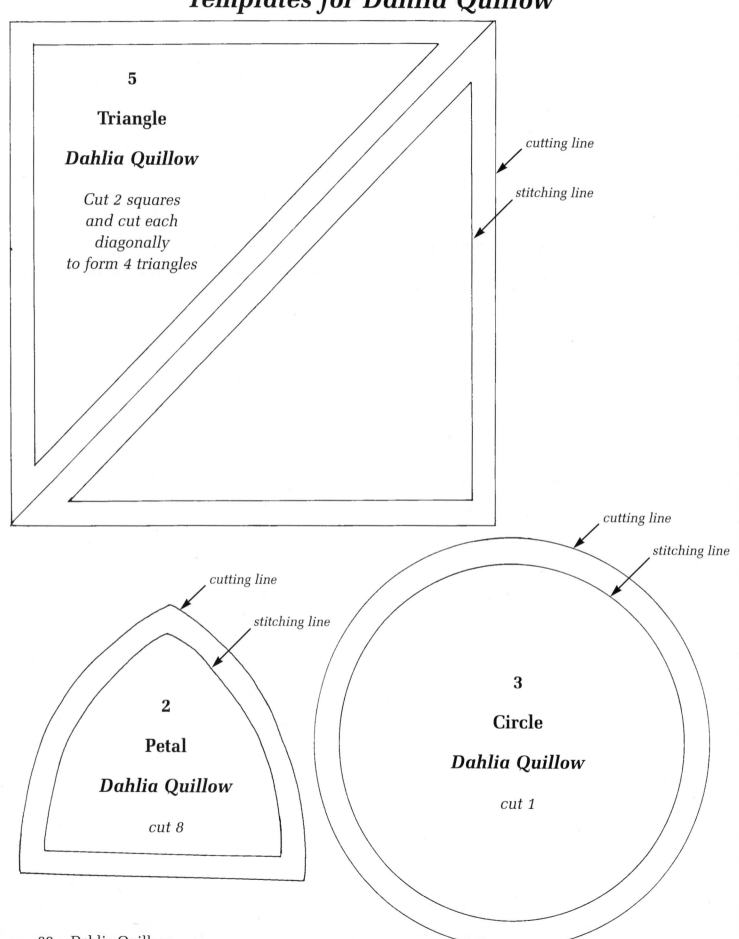

5

Triangle

Dahlia Quillow

*Cut 2 squares
and cut each
diagonally
to form 4 triangles*

cutting line

stitching line

cutting line

stitching line

cutting line

stitching line

2

Petal

Dahlia Quillow

cut 8

3

Circle

Dahlia Quillow

cut 1

Dahlia Table Runner

Finished size is approximately 13" x 53"

Fabric Requirements

Fabric 1—Templates 1, 3, Strip C, back —
1½ yds.

Fabric 2—Template 2, Strip B, binding—
½ yd.

Fabric 3—Strip A—⅛ yd.

Fabric 4—Templates 4, 5, Strip D—¼ yd.

Batting—14" x 54"

The Dahlia patch for the table runner is made up of five shapes which will be identified in the text as follows:

1. Trees (Template 1 on page 84)—
   cut 8 of Fabric 1
2. Petals (Template 2 on page 84)—
   cut 8 of Fabric 2
3. Center (Template 3 on page 84)—
   cut 1 of Fabric 1
4. Squares (Template 4 on page 84)—
   cut 4 of Fabric 4
5. Triangles (Template 5 on page 84)—
   cut 4 of Fabric 4

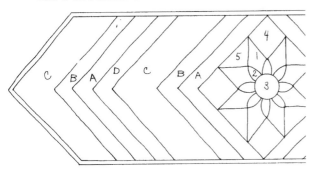

Making the Dahlia Patch

1. Make gathers along the straight edge of the petals. To do so, use a double strand of thread and a medium sized needle. Make a knot at the end of the thread. By hand, begin stitching ¼" from the side edge of the petal and ¼" from the straight edge of the petal.

Make a tiny backstitch at the beginning to secure the knot so it cannot pop through the fabric when you pull the gathers. Make running stitches along the edge, using slightly less than a ¼" seam allowance so the gathering stitches will be hidden in the seam line when the petals are attached to the circle later on.

Pull stitches tightly as you go, creating puckers or gathers in the fabric.

Stitch to ¼" from the other edge of the petal, making enough gathers so that the petal measures ¾" along the straight edge. Make a backstitch and knot the thread to hold the gathers firmly in place. Repeat for all petals.

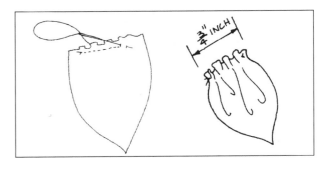

2. Holding the tree so the tip is down and the trunk is up, sew a gathered petal to the left side of each tree curve. Place the petal on top of the tree, right sides together. Pin the petal to the tree at both ends of the curve. Because these pieces are small and curved, you may find it easier to stitch the units together by hand. Begin stitching at the point of the petal and stitch toward the trunk of the tree using a small, tight, running stitch. Ease the fullness of the petal to fit the curve of the tree as you stitch. Clip ⅛" into the curve of the tree if necessary to fit the two pieces together.

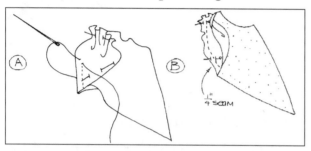

3. Pin triangles onto the right, straight sides of half of the trees so that the long sides of the triangles face the left sides of the trees. Begin stitching at the trunk of each tree and stitch toward the tip. Press the seam toward the tree.

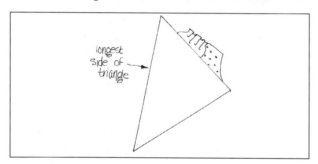

4. Sew squares to the right sides of the remaining trees. Begin sewing at the trunk of each tree and stitch toward the tip. (The tip of the tree will extend slightly beyond the end of the square.) Press the seam toward the tree.

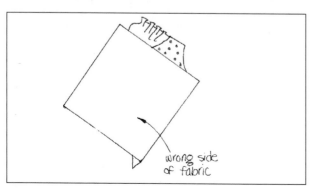

5. Stitch a petal-tree-triangle unit to a petal-tree-square unit. Pin the units together near the center where the petal point meets the tree on one unit and the square meets the tree on the other unit. Have the petal-tree junction and the tree-square junction facing in opposite directions with the seams butted up against each other. Place a pin at this point to assure that the seams meet accurately and cannot shift during stitching. Place a second pin connecting the base of the petal and the trunk of the tree.

Handstitch the petal to the curve of the tree, starting at the base of the tree and stitching to the tip of the petal. Ease the petal to fir the curve, clipping ⅛" into the curve of the tree if necessary to ease the fullness. Handstitch to the tip of the petal. Continue stitching through the pinned joint and through the tree and the triangle. Straight stitching can be done more efficiently by machine. Press the seam toward the tree. Continue the sequence of joining units until the block is completed.

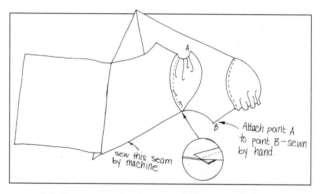

6. Fold the center circle in half and then into quarters to mark it into equal quadrants. Place a pin at each quarter point. Fit the circle into the round opening of the patch, having right sides together and fitting two petals into each quarter of the circle. Pin in place. Stitch around the circle through all thicknesses.

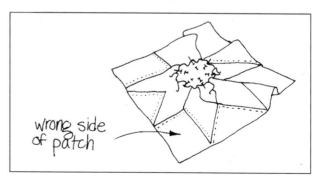

Adding the Strips Around the Dahlia

1. Cut a piece of batting measuring 14" wide x 54" long. Fold the batting in half to mark the center point along two sides.

2. Place the complete Dahlia patch in the center of the batting, aligned with the center of the batting. Pin in place.

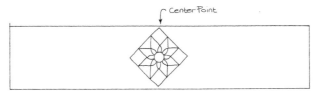

3. Cut two strips of Fabric 1 measuring 3¼" x 45." Cut two strips each of Fabrics 2, 3, and 4, each measuring 2" x 45."

4. With right sides together, pin a 45" strip of Fabric 3 along the top right side of the Dahlia patch. Trim the strip so the end extends just slightly beyond the patch.

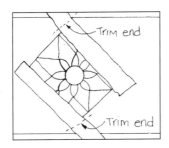

Stitch in place through all thicknesses. Fold out strip and press. Pin the remaining length of the strip to the lower left side of the Dahlia patch. Trim the end so it extends just slightly beyond the patch. Stitch in place through all thicknesses. Fold out the strip and press.

Following the above procedure, use the remaining length of the strip to complete the other two sides of the patch.

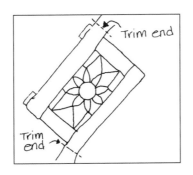

5. Continue building the patch, using the same sequence of attaching strips on top and bottom and then left and right in the following order: Four strips of Fabric 2. Four strips of Fabric 1. Four strips of Fabric 4. Four strips of Fabric 3. Four strips of Fabric 2. Four strips of Fabric 1.

Adding the Backing

1. Trim the batting and the edges of the fabric along each side so the table runner measures 12½" wide. Trim the batting to follow the points at each end of the runner.

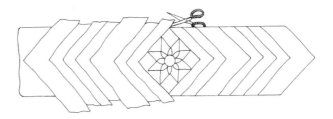

2. Cut the backing from Fabric 1 so it is approximately 1" larger than the pieced top on all sides.

3. Lay the pieced table runner on top of the wrong side of the backing fabric. Pin the top to the back. Stitch close to the edge on all sides. Trim the backing fabric even with the edges of the top.

Binding

1. Cut two binding strips from Fabric 2, each measuring 2" wide and the length of the long side edges of the table runner. Cut four more strips equal in length to the pointed sides on each end plus 2."

2. Fold the binding strips in half lengthwise, wrong sides together, and press. Stitch the binding to the long sides of the table runner through all thicknesses, having the raw edges

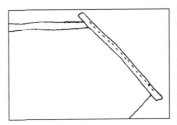

of the binding even with the raw edges of the runner. After the sides are stitched, press the binding out, so that the fold extends beyond the raw edges. Stitch another section of binding along both pointed edges of the ends, stitching through the extended binding along each side. Press out.

3. Fold binding around to the back, encasing all raw edges. Trim excess fabric and fold at corners to create sharp points. Slipstitch in place.

Templates for Dahlia Table Runner

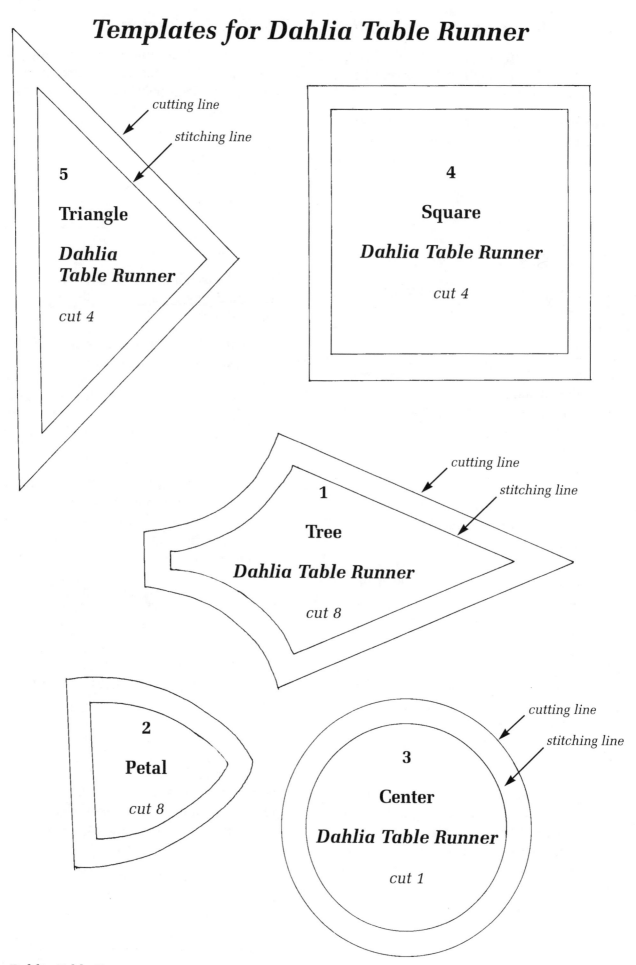

cutting line

stitching line

5

Triangle

Dahlia Table Runner

cut 4

4

Square

Dahlia Table Runner

cut 4

cutting line

stitching line

1

Tree

Dahlia Table Runner

cut 8

2

Petal

cut 8

cutting line

stitching line

3

Center

Dahlia Table Runner

cut 1

Dahlia Placemats

Finished size is approximately 13" x 17"

Fabric Requirements to Make 4 Dahlia Placemats

Fabric 1—Templates 1, 3, Strip C, and backs—1¼ yds.
Fabric 2—Templates 4, 5—¼ yd.
Fabric 3—Template 2, Strip B, binding—⅝ yd.
Fabric 4—Strip A—¼ yd.
Batting—four-14" x 18" pieces

The Dahlia patch is made up of five shapes which will be identified in the text as follows:

1. Trees (Template 1 on page 88)—cut 32 of Fabric 1
2. Petals (Template 2 on page 88)—cut 32 of Fabric 3
3. Circle (Template 3 on page 88)—cut 4 of Fabric 1
4. Squares (Template 4 on page 88)—cut 16 of Fabric 2
5. Triangles (Template 5 on page 88)—cut 16 of Fabric 2

You will need four Dahlia patches to make a set of four placemats.

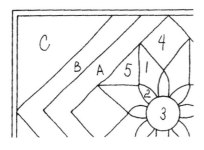

Making the Dahlia Patch

1. Make gathers along the straight edge of the petals. To do so, use a double strand of thread and a medium sized needle. Make a knot at the end of the thread. By hand, begin stitching ¼" from the side edge of the petal and ¼" from the straight edge of the petal.

Make a tiny backstitch at the beginning to secure the knot so it cannot pop through the fabric when you pull the gathers. Make running stitches along the edge, using slightly less than a ¼" seam allowance so the gathering stitches will be hidden in the seam line when the petals are attached to the circle later on.

Pull stitches tightly as you go, creating puckers or gathers in the fabric.

Stitch to ¼" from the other edge of the petal, making enough gathers so that the petal measures ¾" along the straight edge. Make a backstitch and knot the thread to hold the gathers firmly in place. Repeat for all petals.

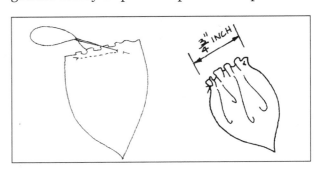

2. Holding the tree so the tip is down and the trunk is up, sew a gathered petal to the left side of each tree curve. Place the petal on top of the tree, right sides together. Pin the petal to the tree at both ends of the curve. Because these pieces are small and curved, you may find it easier to stitch the units together by hand. Begin stitching at the point of the petal and stitch toward the trunk of the tree using a small, tight, running stitch. Ease the fullness of the petal to fit the curve of the tree as you stitch. Clip 1/8" into the curve of the tree if necessary to fit the two pieces together.

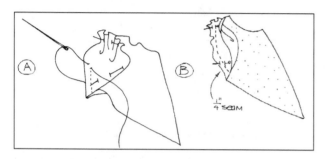

3. Pin triangles onto the right, straight sides of half of the trees so that the long sides of the triangles face the left sides of the trees. Begin stitching at the trunk of each tree and stitch toward the tip. Press the seam toward the tree.

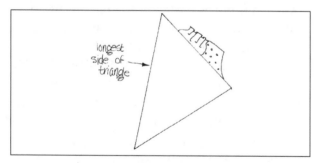

4. Sew squares to the right sides of the remaining trees. Begin sewing at the trunk of each tree and stitch toward the tip. (The tip of the tree will extend slightly beyond the end of the square.) Press the seam toward the tree.

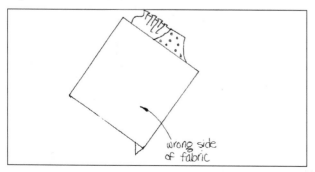

5. Stitch a petal-tree-triangle unit to a petal-tree-square unit. Pin the units together near the center where the petal point meets the tree on one unit and the square meets the tree on the other unit. Have the petal-tree junction and the tree-square junction facing in opposite directions with the seams butted up against each other. Place a pin at this point to assure that the seams meet accurately and cannot shift during stitching. Place a second pin connecting the base of the petal and the trunk of the tree.

Handstitch the petal to the curve of the tree, starting at the base of the tree and stitching to the tip of the petal. Ease the petal to fir the curve, clipping 1/8" into the curve of the tree if necessary to ease the fullness. Handstitch to the tip of the petal. Continue stitching through the pinned joint and through the tree and the triangle. Straight stitching can be done more efficiently by machine. Press the seam toward the tree. Continue the sequence of joining units until the block is completed.

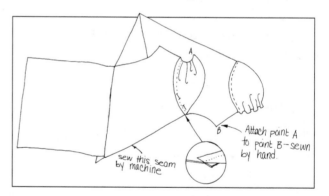

6. Fold the center circle in half and then into quarters to mark it into equal quadrants. Place a pin at each quarter point. Fit the circle into the round opening of the patch, having right sides together and fitting two petals into each quarter of the circle. Pin in place. Stitch around the circle through all thicknesses.

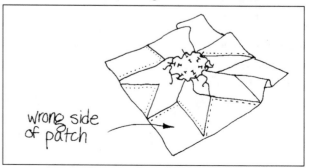

Adding the Strips Around the Dahlia

1. For each placemat, cut a piece of batting measuring 14" x 18." Fold batting in half to mark the center point along each side.

2. Place the complete Dahlia patch in the center of the batting, aligned with the center of the batting. Pin in place.

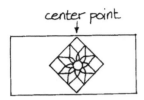

3. Cut four strips of Fabric 1 measuring 5" x 45." Cut four strips each of Fabrics 3 and 4, each measuring 2" x 45."

4. With right sides together, pin a 45" strip of Fabric 4 along the top right side of the Dahlia patch. Trim the strip so the end extends just slightly beyond the patch. Stitch in place through all thicknesses. Fold out the strip and press. Pin the remaining length of the strip to the lower left side of the Dahlia patch. Trim the end so it extends just slightly beyond the patch. Stitch in place through all thicknesses. Fold out the strip and press.

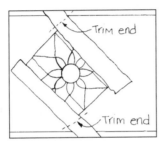

Follow the above procedure, use the remaining length of the strip to complete the other two sides of the patch.

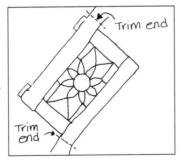

5. Continue building the patch using the same sequence of attaching strips on top and bottom and then left and right in the following order: Four strips of Fabric 3. Four strips of Fabric 1.

Adding the Backing

1. Cut four backs from Fabric 1, each measuring 14" x 19."

2. Center the pieced placemat patch on the backing fabric, having the wrong sides together. Pin the layers together. Baste close to the edge on all sides. Trim backing even with top.

Binding

1. For each placemat, cut 2 binding strips from Fabric 3, 2" wide x 18" long. Cut 2 more binding strips measuring 2" wide x 16" long.

2. Fold the binding strips in half lengthwise and press. Sew the longer binding sections to the long sides of the placemat. Stitch through all thicknesses, having the raw edges of the

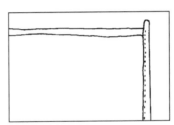

binding even with the raw edges of the pieced placemat. After the long sides are stitched, press the binding out so that the fold extends beyond the raw edges of the placemat.

Sew the shorter binding sections to the ends of the placemat, stitching through the extended binding on both sides. Press out.

3. Fold bindings around to the back and slip-stitch in place, having the fold even with the seam lines. Stitch the sides first and then the ends. Trim excess bulk at corners and fold to create sharp points.

Templates for Dahlia Placemats

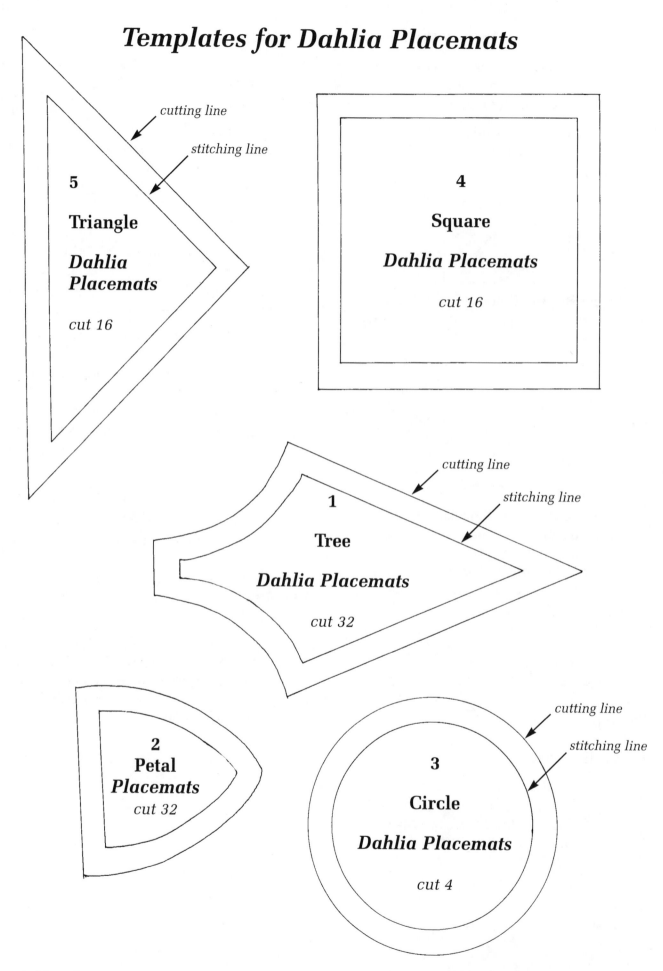

cutting line

stitching line

5

Triangle

Dahlia Placemats

cut 16

4

Square

Dahlia Placemats

cut 16

cutting line

stitching line

1

Tree

Dahlia Placemats

cut 32

2
Petal
Placemats
cut 32

cutting line

stitching line

3

Circle

Dahlia Placemats

cut 4

Dahlia Pillow and Chair Pad

Finished size is approximately 15" (without ruffle)

Fabric Requirements

Fabric 1—Templates 1, 3, ruffle, pillow back—⁷⁄₈ yd.

Fabric 2—Templates 2, 4, 5, ties (for chair pad only)—¹⁄₄ yd.

Batting (for chair pad only)—18" square

Making the Dahlia Patch

The Dahlia patch is made up of five shapes which will be identified in the text as follows:

1. Tree (Template 1, page 92)—cut 8 of Fabric 1
2. Petal (Template 2, page 93)—cut 8 of Fabric 2
3. Circle (Template 3, page 93)—cut 1 of Fabric 1
4. Square (Template 4, page 93)—cut 4 of Fabric 2
5. Triangle (Template 5, page 92)—cut 2 squares of Fabric 2, then cut each diagonally to form 4 triangles

1. Make gathers along the straight edge of the petals. To do so, use a double strand of thread and a medium sized needle. Make a knot at the end of the thread. By hand, begin stitching ¹⁄₄" from the side edge of the petal and ¹⁄₄" from the straight edge of the petal.

Make a tiny backstitch at the beginning to secure the knot so it cannot pop through the fabric when you pull the gathers. Make running stitches along the edge, using slightly less than a ¹⁄₄" seam allowance so the gathering stitches will be hidden in the seam line when the petals are attached to the circle later on.

Pull stitches tightly as you go, creating puckers or gathers in the fabric.

Stitch to ¹⁄₄" from the other edge of the petal, making enough gathers so that the petal

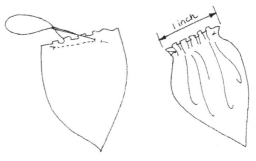

measures 1" along the straight edge. Make a backstitch and knot the thread to hold the gathers firmly in place. Repeat for all petals.

2. Holding the tree so the tip is down and the trunk is up, sew a gathered petal to the left side of each tree curve. Place the petal on top of the tree, right sides together. Pin the petal to the tree at both ends (A). Begin stitching at the point of the petal and stitch toward the tree trunk. Ease the fullness of the petal to fit the curve of the tree as you stitch (B).

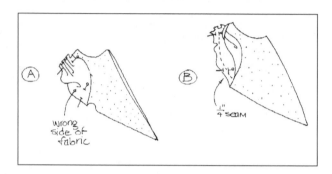

3. Pin triangles onto the right, straight sides of 4 of the trees so that the long sides of the triangles face the left sides of the trees. Begin stitching at the trunk of each tree and stitch toward the tip. Press the seam toward the tree.

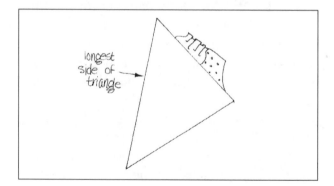

4. Sew squares to the right sides of the remaining 4 trees. Begin sewing at the trunk of each

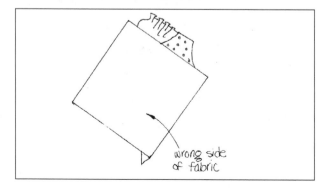

tree and stitch toward the tip. (The tip of the tree will extend slightly beyond the end of the square.) Press the seam toward the tree.

5. Stitch a petal-tree-triangle unit to a petal-tree-square unit. Pin the units together near the center where the petal point meets the tree on one unit and the square meets the tree on the other unit. Have the petal-tree junction and the tree-square junction facing in opposite directions with the seams butted up against each other. Place a pin at this point to assure that the seams meet accurately and cannot shift during stitching. Place a second pin connecting the base of the petal and the trunk of the tree.

With the petal on top, begin stitching at the trunk of the tree, easing the petal to fit the curve. Continue stitching over the pinned joint and through the end of the tree and triangle. Press the seam toward the tree. Continue this sequence until a square patch is completed.

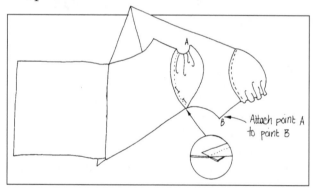

6. Fold the center circle in half and then into quarters to mark it into equal quadrants. Place a pin at each quarter point. Fit the circle into the round opening of the patch, having right sides together and fitting two petals into each quarter of the circle. Pin in place. Stitch around the circle through all thicknesses.

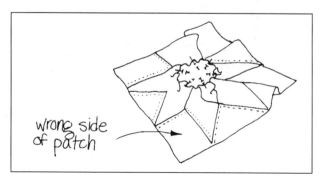

Making a Ruffle

1. Cut three strips of Fabric 1, each 4½" wide x 45" long. Sew the three strips together end to end to make one continuous length. Stitch the two ends together to form a large circle.

2. Fold the fabric in half lengthwise, wrong sides together, to form a 2¼" width of fabric, having raw edges even. Stitch along the entire length of the raw edge with large basting stitches.

3. Pull the thread to form gathers in the ruffle. Ruffle the fabric until it is equal in circumference to the four edges of the pieced patch.

4. Pin the ruffle to the right side of the pieced patch, having the raw edges even and the folded edge of the ruffle facing the center of the patch. Baste the ruffle in place.

raw edge

Adding the Back

1. Cut a backing square from Fabric 1, the same size as the pieced pillow top. Place it, right sides together, on top of the pieced patch with the ruffle sandwiched between the layers.

2. Stitch the back and pieced patch together through all thicknesses, leaving a 5" opening along one side for stuffing.

3. Turn the pillow right side out and stuff. Slipstitch the opening.

Instructions for Making a Dahlia Chair Pad

1. Prepare a Dahlia Patch and ruffle as explained on pages 89-91.

2. Cut four strips from Fabric 2, each measuring 2" x 15."

3. Fold under and press down ½" on both long edges and one end of each strip. Fold the strip in half lengthwise, encasing all raw edges, and stitch along the open edge and across the folded end. Repeat with the other three strips.

4. Place two ties at each of two corners of one edge of the chair pad. Keep the raw edge of the ties even with the raw edge of the pieced top and basted ruffle, and the "tails" of the ties toward the center. Baste the ties in place.

Adding Batting

1. Cut a square of batting the same size as the pieced chair pad top.

2. Place the batting against the wrong side of the pieced top. Baste in place.

Adding the Back

1. Cut a backing square from Fabric 1 the same size as the pieced top and batting. Place it, right sides together, over the pieced patch with the ruffle and the ties sandwiched between the layers. Pin securely.

2. Stitch through all the layers, allowing a 5" opening along one edge for turning.

3. Turn the chair pad right side out. Slip-stitch the opening.

Optional Quilting

The chair pad may be hand or machine quilted, outlining the Dahlia patch.

Templates for Dahlia Pillow or Chair Pad

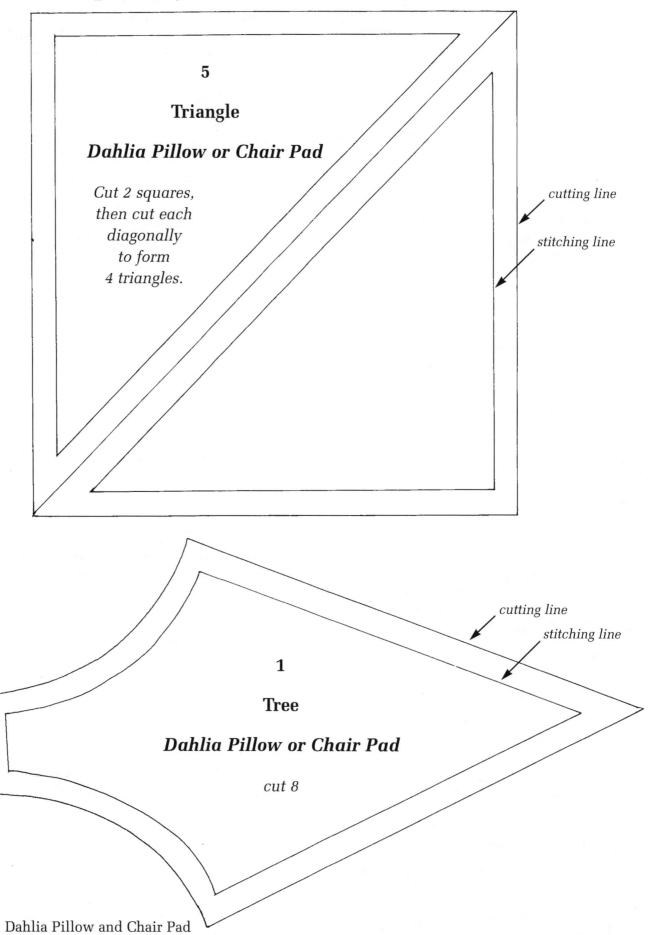

5

Triangle

Dahlia Pillow or Chair Pad

*Cut 2 squares,
then cut each
diagonally
to form
4 triangles.*

cutting line

stitching line

cutting line

stitching line

1

Tree

Dahlia Pillow or Chair Pad

cut 8

Templates for Dahlia Pillow or Chair Pad

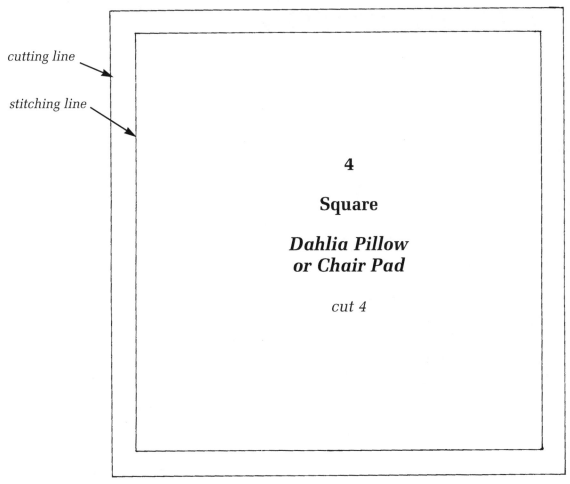

cutting line

stitching line

4

Square

Dahlia Pillow or Chair Pad

cut 4

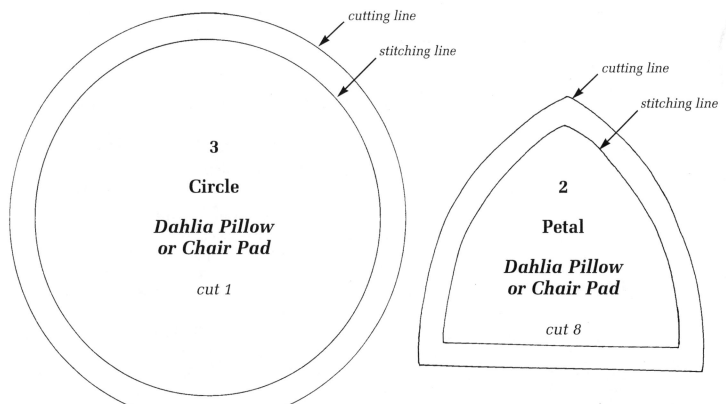

cutting line

stitching line

3

Circle

Dahlia Pillow or Chair Pad

cut 1

cutting line

stitching line

2

Petal

Dahlia Pillow or Chair Pad

cut 8

Dahlia Apron

Fabric Requirements

Fabric 1—Templates 1, 3, skirt, neck ties, waist ties, waistband—1 yd.

Fabric 2—Strip A, back of apron bib, pocket—½ yd.

Fabric 3—Template 2—¹⁄₁₆ yd.

Fabric 4—Templates 4, 5—⅛ yd.

Batting—one-12" square

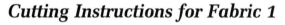

Cutting Instructions for Fabric 1

1. Cut 2 neck tie pieces, each measuring 3" wide x 21" long.

2. Cut 1 apron skirt measuring 45" wide x 23" long.

3. Cut 2 waist ties, each measuring 3" wide x 30" long.

4. Cut 2 waistband strips, each measuring 3" wide x 21" long.

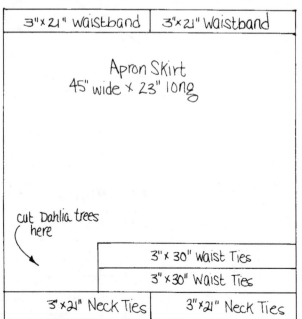

Cutting Instructions for Fabric 2

1. Cut two strips, each 2" wide x width of Dahlia patch, for the top and bottom borders on bib.

2. Cut two strips, each 2" wide x height of Dahlia patch plus top and bottom borders, for left and right borders on bib.

3. Cut back of apron bib to exact size of Dahlia patch plus border strips.

4. Cut one pocket 5½" wide x 7" high.

Making the Dahlia Patch

The Dahlia patch is made up of five shapes which will be identified in the text as follows:

1. Trees (Template 1, page 98)—cut 8 of Fabric 1
2. Petals (Template 2, page 98)—cut 8 of Fabric 3
3. Circle (Template 3, page 98)—cut 1 of Fabric 1
4. Squares (Template 4, page 98)—cut 4 of Fabric 4
5. Triangles (Template 5, page 98)—cut 4 of Fabric 4

1. Make gathers along the straight edge of the petals. To do so, use a double strand of thread and a medium sized needle. Make a knot at the end of the thread. By hand, begin stitching ¼" from the side edge of the petal and ¼" from the straight edge of the petal.

Make a tiny backstitch at the beginning to secure the knot so it cannot pop through the fabric when you pull the gathers. Make running stitches along the edge, using slightly less than a ¼" seam allowance so the gathering stitches will be hidden in the seam line when the petals are attached to the circle later on.

Pull stitches tightly as you go, creating puckers or gathers in the fabric.

Stitch to ¼" from the other edge of the petal, making enough gathers so that the petal measures ¾" along the straight edge. Make a backstitch and knot the thread to hold the gathers firmly in place. Repeat for all petals.

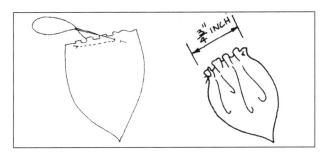

2. Holding the tree so the tip is down and the trunk is up, sew a gathered petal to the left side of each tree curve. Place the petal on top of the tree, right sides together. Pin the petal to the tree at both ends of the curve. Because these pieces are small and curved, you may find it easier to stitch the units together by hand. Begin stitching at the point of the petal and stitch toward the trunk of the tree using a small, tight, running stitch. Ease the fullness of the petal to fit the curve of the tree as you stitch. Clip ⅛" into the curve of the tree if necessary to fit the two pieces together.

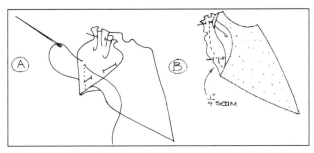

3. Pin triangles onto the right, straight sides of half of the trees so that the long sides of the triangles face the left sides of the trees. Begin stitching at the trunk of each tree and stitch toward the tip. Press the seam toward the tree.

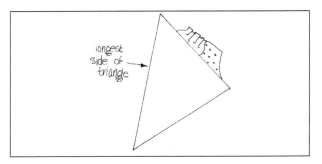

4. Sew squares to the right sides of the remaining trees. Begin sewing at the trunk of each tree and stitch toward the tip. (The tip of the tree will extend slightly beyond the end of the square.) Press the seam toward the tree.

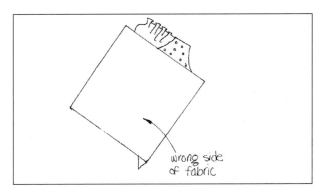

5. Stitch a petal-tree-triangle unit to a petal-tree-square unit. Pin the units together near the center where the petal point meets the tree on one unit and the square meets the tree on the other unit. Have the petal-tree junction and the tree-square junction facing in opposite directions with the seams butted up against each other. Place a pin at this point to assure that the seams meet accurately and cannot shift during stitching. Place a second pin connecting the base of the petal and the trunk of the tree.

Handstitch the petal to the curve of the tree, starting at the base of the tree and stitching to the tip of the petal. Ease the petal to fir the curve, clipping ⅛" into the curve of the tree if necessary to ease the fullness. Handstitch to the tip of the petal. Continue stitching through the pinned joint and through the tree and the triangle. (Straight stitching can be done more efficiently by machine.) Press the seam toward the tree. Continue the sequence of joining units until the block is completed.

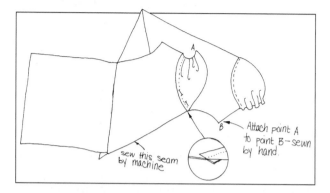

6. Fold the center circle in half and then into quarters to mark it into equal quadrants. Place a pin at each quarter point. Fit the circle into the round opening of the patch, having right sides together and fitting two petals into each quarter of the circle. Pin in place. Stitch around the circle through all thicknesses.

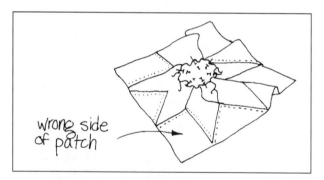

Making the Bib of the Apron

1. Cut a piece of batting measuring 12" square. Center the Dahlia patch on the batting and pin in place.

2. Take the top and bottom border strips and lay one strip across the top of the patch, with right sides together and raw edges even. Pin in place through the strip, patch, and batting. Stitch in place through all layers. Repeat along the bottom edge using the second strip. Press strips out.

3. Take the left and right border strips and lay these two strips along each side, right sides together and raw edges even. Pin and stitch through all layers. Press strips out. Trim away any excess batting along the edges.

Making the Neck Ties

1. Fold the two neck tie strips in half lengthwise, right sides together. Using a ¼" seam allowance, stitch along one end and the long side of both strips. Let the other end open for turning. Turn strips right side out. Press.

2. Lay the Dahlia patch on a flat surface with the right side facing you. Place the ties along the top side of the patch so that the raw, open ends of the ties are even with the top of the patch and the seam of the tie is even with the seam of the strip on the Dahlia patch. Pin in place. Gather the ties together near the center of the patch so they will not get caught in seams when attaching the back of the patch.

3. Place the back over the patch with right sides together and with the wrong side facing you. Pin the layers together. Stitch along both sides and the top using a ¼" seam allowance. Turn patch right side out.

4. Place the apron bib between the two waistband strips with right sides together, raw edges even along the lower edge, and the bib in the center of the waistband. Stitch along the edge of the waistband through all thicknesses. Press seam toward waistband.

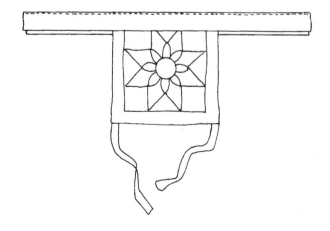

Making the Pocket

1. Fold under and stitch a ¼" seam allowance along the top edge of the pocket.

2. Fold under 1" along the top edge of the pocket and press in place.

3. Fold under ½ inch along the bottom and sides of the pocket. Stitch close to the edge along the sides and bottom.

4. Position the pocket on the apron skirt, having the outer edge of the pocket 10" from the side of the skirt and the bottom of the pocket 10" from the lower edge of the skirt. Stitch the pocket in place along the sides and bottom, stitching close to the edge and near the previous pocket stitching.

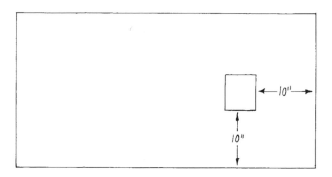

Making the Apron Skirt

1. Fold under and press ¼" along the lower edge and both sides of the apron skirt. Fold again to encase the raw edges and stitch, using a ¼" seam allowance.

2. Stitch ¼" from the top edge along the top of the apron skirt using a long running stitch. Stitch again close to the prior stitching. Pull the threads to gather the top edge of the skirt until it measures 20" in width. Spread gathers evenly.

Adding the Bib and Waistband

1. Fold under ½" along the lower edge of the back waistband. Press in place.

2. Fold the apron skirt in half from side to side to find the center point of the gathered edge. Do the same with the waistband. With right sides together, pin the unturned edge of the waistband to the gathered skirt, having the center points aligned. The waistband should extend ½" beyond the skirt on each end. Stitch the waistband to the skirt using a ½" seam allowance. Press the seam toward the waistband.

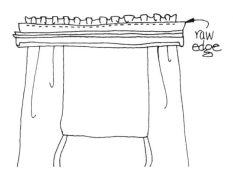

3. Make the waistband ties by folding each strip in half lengthwise, right sides together. Using a ¼" seam allowance, stitch along one end and the long side of both strips. Let the other end open for turning. Turn strips right side out. Press.

4. Place a waistband tie between the waistband at each end, so that the open end of the tie is even with the end of the waistband. Center the tie in the waistband. Stitch the ends of the waistband using a ½" seam allowance.

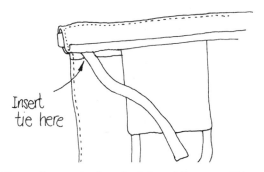

Insert tie here

5. Turn the waistband right side out. Slip-stitch the folded edge of the waistband to the apron skirt at the seam line, encasing the raw edges.

Templates for Dahlia Apron

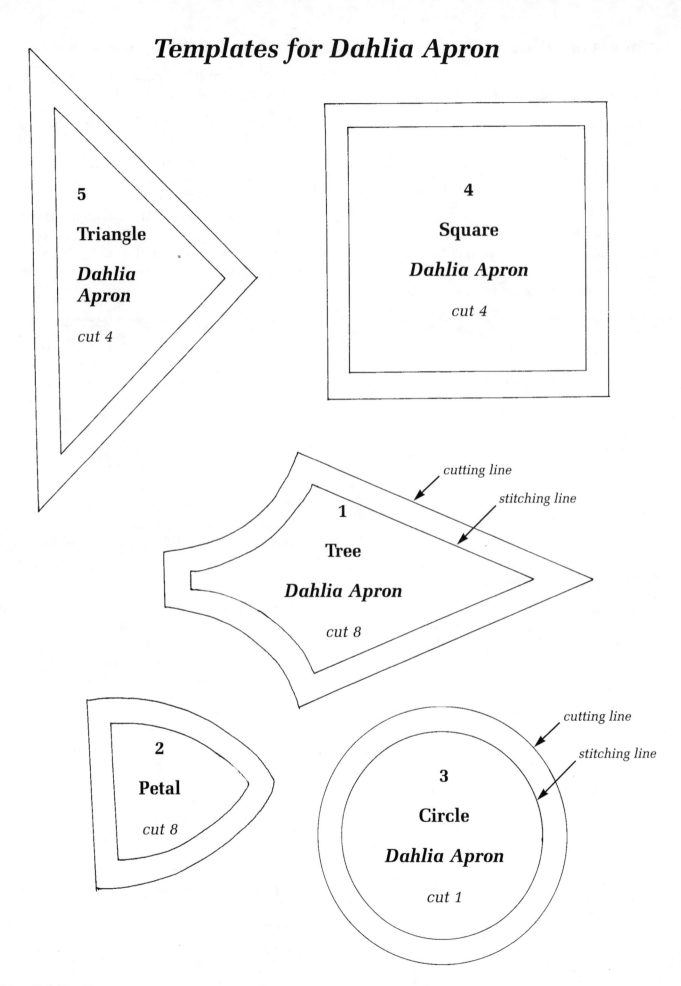

5

Triangle

Dahlia Apron

cut 4

4

Square

Dahlia Apron

cut 4

cutting line

stitching line

1

Tree

Dahlia Apron

cut 8

2

Petal

cut 8

cutting line

stitching line

3

Circle

Dahlia Apron

cut 1